HUMAN CAPITAL DILEMMA

LI**A**BLE TO EMPLOYEES,
LI**A**BILITY TO ORGANIZATION

TUHIN BISWAS

notionpress.com

INDIA · SINGAPORE · MALAYSIA

Notion Press

No.8, 3rd Cross Street
CIT Colony, Mylapore
Chennai, Tamil Nadu – 600004

First Published by Notion Press 2020
Copyright © Tuhin Biswas 2020
All Rights Reserved.

ISBN 978-1-64951-790-6

This book has been published with all efforts taken to make the material error-free after the consent of the author. However, the author and the publisher do not assume and hereby disclaim any liability to any party for any loss, damage, or disruption caused by errors or omissions, whether such errors or omissions result from negligence, accident, or any other cause.

While every effort has been made to avoid any mistake or omission, this publication is being sold on the condition and understanding that neither the author nor the publishers or printers would be liable in any manner to any person by reason of any mistake or omission in this publication or for any action taken or omitted to be taken or advice rendered or accepted on the basis of this work. For any defect in printing or binding the publishers will be liable only to replace the defective copy by another copy of this work then available.

Contents

Introduction	5
Chapter 1: HR Does What CEO/Mgmt Wants Them to Do…	9
# A Brief……	9
# CEO Who Thinks HR Is a Liability and Good for Nothing	12
# How Can HR Head Develop a Good Rapport with CEO/CXO's	15
Chapter 2: How Can HR Come Out of the Sandwich Position (between Employer/Management and Employee) and Perform a Clear Mindset Job Role	23
# A Brief……	23
# Positive Conflicts - Speaks about good fights for a organizational gain. 6 tactics of +Ve conflicts.	24
# Fighting Teams - Developing teams that have positive fighting spirits	27
# What and How do you communicate to develop positive mindset.	28
# The Art of Persuasion - If there ever was a time for business leaders to learn the fine art of persuasion, it is now.	63
# Resilient Leadership - Resilient individuals are able to sustain successful performance and positive wellbeing in the face of adverse conditions and to recover from or adjust easily to misfortune or change.	64

Chapter 3: HR Doesn't Understand Business Expectations   81

    # Inside CEO's Mind? What is CEO thinking on people's business function   84

    # What Business Wants? Expectations of CXOs from Business...   90

    # Digitization across functions   129

    # Leaders to define path...   154

Chapter 4: Where Should We Head To?   163

    # A World of Trust and Being Human   163

    # New Dimension... The world is changing...   183

    # I will get there!...... What it takes to reach my goal...   186

    # Way to growth...... Don't miss enjoying journey, destination is near by...   191

Industry Perspective   *197*

Conclusion   *203*

References   *205*

Introduction

Dedicated to all my friends in Human resources. Who loves this profession of Human being dealing with Human beings...

Early morning at 8 am on a Sunday, sipping a cup of Tea during Covid19 lockdown, was thinking about how would the jobs change post Covid19 due to pandemic recession across the world. Few Experts say the most affected functions will be those which have less customer interface or direct interface to revenue of the organization, so-called non-core jobs. One of the function which is very important but still considered as cost function is Human resources.

So thought let me write a book on my function the people function/human resources function as there will be lots and lots of ups and downs, challenges with this function now and in the coming years. As Hassan Choughari says "The hardest challenge being an HR is that sometimes you have to be the LAWYER, the JUDGE, and the HANGMAN."

From the last few months I had been getting calls from many CEO/HR Heads/Entrepreneurs from startup to Big companies on how to manage people/HR Costs/productivity etc in such sensitive times. Somewhere I felt the crisis has come and everyone now got a chance to retrench people or restructure the organization. A few of my know people in HR also called me in anticipation of losing jobs. This is not been happening now, from the last 2 years I see a lot of frustration in HR Leaders and also with CEO'S/CXO's on HR delivery. While there has been a good amount of churn in HR professionals/leaders, few ventured to start consulting on their own, few ventured into different businesses, etc. Meanwhile, even Management/CEOs also have been looking for reliable and able HR leaders to guide and advise them on people's strategy, but sometimes find it difficult to get the right person.

This book will make you aware of few practical issues you face in your day to day work lives, the dilemma you face with management and employee, how can we become an able business HR leader, and few worth solutions you can deal with.

About me, I never thought I will be in human resources function or make HR as my career. It was destined to become a Doctor I had also got a merit seat in a well known Medical college but Kismat (Fate) had a different story.

I have been in HR for the last 20 plus years working for MNC's and corporate houses at senior leadership positions. While I have worked with various sectors like FMCG, Infrastructure, logistics, etc what I see is, some trends are common across sectors particularly when it comes to managing management and employees. It may differ a bit based on the organization whether it is a service sector or manufacturing but the underline principles are more or less the same as we deal with humans.

Is it true **HR does what Management wants them to do…?**. Most of the HR leaders who I have spoken say that yes to a large extend because no one wants a confrontation with Management and end of the day they have to do things that save their job. This is a big debatable question. We will talk more about this in my book. This would be my first element

The second main topic is **How can HR come out of the sandwich position and perform a clear mindset job role?**. We have seen many a times that HR is sandwiched between Management and employees. As an HR professional you may sometimes feel that employees has a point of view and maybe they are right, but when the employees proposal is taken to management it can be shot down for various reasons. Vice versa. Sometimes Management has a proposal, maybe like a retrenchment plan or so, now you as HR have to communicate the pink slip theory to employees which may not be a nice work to do. This will be my second topic which will be deliberated in chapter two.

You must have heard from many business leaders and functional leaders as HR doesn't understand business expectations and doesn't deliver as per management needs. So the third element that I'm going to speak in this book is about **"Business leaders expectation from HR and What will make HR guys as good Business-oriented leaders.**

Chapter Four is about, **Where should we head to**?. After understanding the main crux of first three chapters, it is essential for us to know, what is laid ahead of us. Four relevant topic which i spoke here are

A World of Trust and Being Human , # New Dimension... The world is changing... , # I will get there!...... What it take to reach my goal...

Way to growth...... Don't miss enjoying journey, destination is near by..

This Book is written in very soft and under-stable language with not too many jargons at all. It can be read and digested well by all leaders

– **Tuhin Biswas**

1

HR Does What CEO/Mgmt Wants Them to Do…

A Brief……

The CHRO/head of HR is frequently, at least in the CEO's eyes, seen as the low man (or woman) on the executive totem pole. This occurs even though *people* are the biggest item on almost every company's budget, and that CEOs Consistently list talent as a top concern.

While CEOs may preach an equal playing field among the executive team, that's not always the case. Those who are closest to the money will be placed higher up the ladder (CFOs, finance directors, heads of sales etc.), leaving Human resource head/CHRO's near the bottom rung.

We can all agree that HR is undeniably important, but being a leadership afterthought is still a reality for many HR professionals, and it's worth looking at why this is the case.

"Rarely do we hear people asking, 'Should the finance director be at the executive table?' But often we hear this about HR. I see myself as a member of the executive team, with a technical expertise in HR, in the same way a finance director is a member of the executive team with a technical expertise in finance

A new study revealed that there was 16% higher CHRO turnover rate in 2019 versus 2018 at Fortune 200 companies. They found that about one in five CHROs were replaced last year, with larger firms more likely to see a turnover than smaller firms. The study determined the reason why: a change in CEO directly impacted CHRO turnover. Findings also showed that internal succession of CHROs continue to be on the decline. On how CEO turnover impacted the top HR role, Talent Strategy Group found that of the 35 new CEOs who got the job in 2019, 40% replaced their CHROs. This was especially apparent in 2019 as there was a 40% increase in CEO turnover that year, compared with 2018. Where the CEO hails from also impacted succession plans. An internal CEO successor was 2.5 times more likely to replace the current CHRO in 2019. However, they're more likely to look for a replacement from within the company. Almost three in five internal CEOs replaced the role with an internal CHRO successor. This compares with external CEO candidates, who only appointed someone from within the company 33% of the time. Overall, internal CHRO succession strategies have been on a steady decline. 2019 saw the lowest rate of internal CHRO promotions at 53% appointments. The figure was 61% in 2018, and 70% in 2017.

When a CEO and CHRO work together effectively, the whole business feels the impact. But the same can be said for those who don't work together well.

Imagine a scenario where an organisation's chief HR officer and chief executive officer engage in a popularity contest. The CHRO is jealous of the CEO and vying for their job; the CEO feels threatened and is accused of bullying the CHRO. Trust is eroded, the relationship crumbles and, as a result, everyone in the organisation suffers.

This example, albeit extreme, shows just how bad things can get when HR and the CEO don't align on important matters. There are many reasons these relationships can fail: a stubborn leader, a personality clash, an assumption that HR doesn't add enough value or an organisation rooted in the past. But one thing is sure: when the CEO and HR lead are on the same page, it makes a world of difference.

I have seen that most of the CEO's being the head of the Business would like to be visible, which is good and has to be. But many a times we see HR playing a submissive role, it may be either he has been treated like this or he himself feels being submissive because of his not profit function. CEO's mind set has to change and they should start appreciating the contributions of HR and build a strong bonding for better organizational relations. HR head should also thrive to push/convenience/influence CEO of his existence and what difference he can make to the organization.

I take the liberty to say CEO and CHRO is like a husband wife relationship, they have to complement on each other. When it works it sets example for impeccable leadership and when it doesn't work it becomes a biggest failure like divorces in marriage. Which leaves sour taste at both the ends? CEO should realize that if anyone is going to make me popular among employees is the HR leader, as at least 60 percentage of CEO's role is people management

As we know it is very much important to Align HR goals with Business goals/Organizational goals, sometimes it so happens that even though your HR strategy is well defined, well planned, your strategy/planning can be discarded when the proposal is brought in front of the leadership team.

And many times the function that has a SAY in the organization, the CEO eventually tends to the leader of that function as he may feel after all the other function leader is important for the organization than the HR Head. You are either asked to modify or come up with new thoughts. I don't say the thoughts of other leaders are not up to the mark, but it can't be that most of the time it is an attitude of I say you do. Since senior management feels HR is a cost and not revenue generator you are most of the time cornered. May not be always and not in all cases, But I have also seen organization where HR is respected and are part of major decision of the organization. The CEO's/leadership team can do few basic things to provide a level of comfortlessness among HR leaders by showing respect, challenge them on their thoughts, encourage them to learn, gain knowledge more in business, Be part of HR meetings, etc.

Management also should be aware of how to deal with HR folks to demonstrated productivity or to take the best of them. We take care of sales guys or customer interface employees so well then why not HR guys who are responsible for internal customer satisfaction. **It is a pity that HR employees who are liable for employee engagement and to keep employees motivated and productive become a liability to Organizations.** If the organization wants to grow and be healthy it is important to invest in the right HR talent, find ways to motivate them, hear them out so that they can help Management/Organizations perform better. On the contrary how can HR folks demand respect and not feel that they only do what management wants them to do? Let me tell you two stories related to this challenge.

CEO Who Thinks HR Is a Liability and Good for Nothing

Story one is the story of a CEO who thinks HR is a liability and good for nothing. A senior HR Leader named Ravi joined this organization where the above person was the CEO. He got fed-up within a few weeks of joining as CEO who interviewed him was different now. He uses to always disrespect and insult for small issues. Ravi feels the CEO doesn't listen at all and gets into unnecessary arguments and finally says do as he says. Whatever position you are in the organization, if your boss is not good you lose interested even though you have joined the best organization. A person leaves bosses and not the organization. He was worried but never gave up, so he started finding more information about his boss, why was he reacting like this and why his behavior keeps changing particularly when it comes to HR professionals. After doing some good research Ravi found out that his boss was once upon a time fired for the reasons which had something to do with HR and he also got to know that he was not treated well. He was jobless for a year. This made him develop an ill feeling about HR professionals' weather it may be senior or junior. Once Ravi understood the issue he started his approach to CEO differently. Finally he could see some improvement in their relationships. Not all cases have history but the mindset of looking beyond has to improve.

I have seen over the years that many of the senior management/CEO's go through different not so good experience which reflects in their jobs. This creates an instability/blame game situation among the management group and then the functional managers start working in silos to avoid conflicts.

Vivekananda once said blame none for your faults/experiences and when there is a conflict between the heart and the brain, let the heart be followed.

Some people always indulge in bitterly blaming, others when they fail to achieve a goal. This negative attitude of blame game prevents them from looking at themselves with introspection and to take corrective steps for the failure. Swamiji impresses Mrs. H.G.Wale to stay away from blaming others through his letter which says "I am firmly persuaded that a man is never improved by abuse but by the praise, and so with nations. He also says send few goods words instead of abuse, that will make our people love for America and if you can't at least cease from abusing them.

Sri Ramakrishna Paramahamsa used to describe a story to highlight the futility of blaming others. A monk lived in front of a temple and a prostitute also happened to live in a nearby house. The monk used to always abuse, blame the prostitute for the work she uses to do instead of indulging in spiritual activities. He used to throw one stone in front of the house to count every visitor that entered the prostitute's house. And when it became big heap he used to severely reprimand the prostitute showing the heap of stones which signified her sins. By hearing the words of the monk, the prostitute felt very sorry and sincerely prayed to God every day to forgive her sins. God listened to the sincere prayers of the prostitute. One day the prostitute died and coincidentally even the Monk died the same day. Monk went to hell and the prostitute went to heaven. Noticing that the Monk started raising his voice stating that the act of God was not justifiable. God said clarifying him that the prostitute prayed to God every day sincerely for her inability while the monk indulged in blaming the prostitute every day and never cared to devote his time for praying to God. The verdict of God was right and justified.

Never talk about the faults of others, no matter how bad they may be, Nothing is ever gained by that. You never help one by talking about his fault: you do him an injury and injure yourself as well.

The other thing which Corporate Managers or leaders should follow is that most of the time they should follow heart than mind. When there is a conflict between the heart and the brain, let the heart be followed. Your decisions from the heart are always genuine and you may not get into a problem so easily unless something is going illegally wrong.

A incident something similar. In one of my company which I was working as Head HR, we use to often go through Industrial relations issues. In 2016 we were negotiating with the union for their three-year wage settlement. As usual the demands of Union were high and the company wasn't doing so well in terms of profitability from the past three years. We tried negotiating hard to give them a reasonable increase, all charter of demand points were more or less done except the final wage increase negotiation. We presented much data to them in-terms of increases given in other similar sector companies, inflations, what have management invested in working conditions of employees, benefits over the years, etc. But they were not convinced. Management/board was quite worried if they go on sabotage, go-slow tactics or notice for a strike, etc. We then started talking to Union leaders, individual plant leaders, and employees about the financial conditions of the company and how we were struggling to sell our products in the market. HR dept started communicating with an open heart to the organization without any hidden agenda. It is Human nature that when you start communicating from heart, people notice the genuine intentions. After continuous dialogues for few days, union employees understood that our concerns were genuine and the company wouldn't deprive of getting benefits to employees when it does well. Union got convinced and we finally could see a good negotiation that went through with a win-win situation. So using heart over mind acts most of the time well.

How Can HR Head Develop a Good Rapport with CEO/CXO's

My second story is a little different. Here i have spoken about how can HR professionals build competence to develop a good rapport with CEO/CXO's. One of my well know friend who is again a senior HR professional named Sameer (Name changed) came to me one day and said he is quitting the job because he often is targeted and because of which he lands up with not so good conversations with his CEO, he says the CEO doesn't listen to me at all, whenever I propose he rejects saying this is not up to the mark. He then concludes saying "just do what I said". Because of the CEO's attitude towards him, the entire

Management team feels the HR Head/HR team is useless. Before giving solutions I asked him a few questions like

How is your working relationship with your reporting Manager, in this case, it was CEO. His answer to the first question was not so good as he always feels threatened and the CEO is always finding fault in him. Then I asked him is it the same way from the day you joined, he says no but eventually, he develops some kind of hat redness for HR function and me. See in any organization you join or the level in which you join the first few months you have to spend developing rapport with your boss of course, your team and your peers. This is the most important task which you should do. Now how do I build rapport with my boss and peer group?

When you are hired you are liked by Management, so the first step of **Being liked** is done. The next step is **Spend Quality time** with CEO and peers to show your urge/inquisitiveness about the company function, challenges, etc. The third aspect would be How do you get **respected for your profession** here you have to do few things to the functions like most critical but quick wins once which you can solve, do that so that functional leaders can develop confidence in you. Step into a situation to give your support. This good deed goes to CEO's ears and that develops confidence in you. Remember CEO will only like you, if he hears good things about you in the organization particularly from his direct reports. The fourth one is, CXO's need to **admire your "whole person"**—not just who you are at work. This only happens as your relationship begins to migrate in the workplace and also outside the workplace. Over time, as you get to know people better, other aspects of their life become part of the conversation. Are you active in church or charity? Do you volunteer? If you have children, how much time do you spend with them? Are you living a life worthy of others' respect? Once this step has been accomplished, the other person will be *genuinely* happy and interested to hear of your success and accomplishments. There will be no resentment or jealously. And the 5th one is when you are looked as **an advisor/guide** soon. Once you can solve quick wins, and start building a relationship with Peers, they will start relying on you for there HR problems and good solutions, keep doing that it need not be a right solution always but the intend of solving should always be there.

This is how you should build rapport, I said to Sameer. He agreed that somehow he was busy solving the HR problems of the organization and so couldn't much concentrate on rapport building.

The second question that I asked him was. **How well do you understand the organizational need?** He said fair enough. When you say you have a fair understanding of Business, I doubt whether the person knows the business pain points or HR pain points. Hence thought of advising him what HR should do when it comes to the understanding of organizational needs.

It is a well-known fact that there is no unique Management structure that all Organizations follow. Even though different organizations follow different types of Management structures, (maybe with differentiated function or department names) it could be depicted in a generalized form. However HR should have a wider knowledge of the main functions which are found in any type of organization. Within a highly competitive, rapidly changing, demand-driven business environment, the Sales & Marketing function has a greater role to play. In understanding this role in respect of a particular organization, the first step for HR will be identifying the products or services and the target market. Depending on the nature of the product or services of the organization, activities, processes & strategies could be different. In most of the cases, the Sales & Marketing workforces are managed differently. Their training needs, performance measurement, incentive structures could be very specific. However HR professionals should be able to cater, not only the current, even the future needs of this Sales & marketing function. Without the knowledge of these integral aspects of the function, HR will not be able to serve the changing needs. Similarly HR professionals should understand other functions of its challenges and strategies and how can HR support to mitigate challenges Therefore HR professionals are required to be ready for the future organizational strategy changes by knowing where the business is directed.

And the next question which I asked him was **how collaborative are you with your functional heads!** He said yes I think so, I had been doing my job well. I have always catered what functional needs for human resource deliveries. But that is not exactly what collaboration is? The manager feels they collaborate well or are they failing to understand the word collaboration. Leaders, Managers, employees, business people today are working more collaboratively than ever before, not just inside companies but also with suppliers, customers, governments, and universities. Global virtual teams are the norms, not the exception. Facebook, Twitter, LinkedIn, video conferencing, and host of technologies have put connectivity on steroids and enabled new forms of collaboration that would have been impossible sometimes ago.

Many executives realize that they need a new playbook for this hyper-connected environment. Those who climbed the corporate ladder in silos while using a "command and control" style can have a difficult time adjusting to the new realities. Conversely the Manager who tries to lead by consensus can quickly see decision making and execution grind to a halt. Crafting the right leadership style isn't easy. The best performing CEO's/CXO's/HR Heads are the best to collaborate. I was reading an article of Harvard Business Reviews and hence told Sameer what I experienced with the understanding of collaboration. There are few steps which I spoke about

Do I connect well - A good connector can link people, ideas, and resources that wouldn't normally bump into one another. In business, connectors are critical facilitators of collaboration. While it is true for all Managers but as an HR Head it is very important that you continuously connect to other functional heads and their teams to make your existence felt. The connection need not be only on HR topics it can be on any topic and any time during lunch, casual meet, and many more.

Deep dive to engage – It is not sufficient for you only to collaborate, you should also engage your peers to collaborate. Collaborative leadership is the capacity to engage people and groups outside one's formal control and inspire them to work toward common goals. Let me tell you a story of my own.

When I was working for an FMCG company for all most 9 years, when I joined the company I saw we were working in silos wearing the only functional cap and nowhere anyone was bothered on big organizational issues and spend time on critical thinking on business growth. Everyone had different views and most of the time we went on and on for many meetings without any conclusive outcome. Our MD and I were very worried as we didn't see any collaboration across the organization and the organization suffered. While we new our challenges and individual needs we couldn't find a proper solution. Bur after many deliberations we have decided to take our management through the Strategic Leadership program with IMD for 2 years, it was an intense program but lots to do on case studies, teamwork, collaborative study, and leadership lessons. My MD and I continuously monitored improvements, involved functional heads for collaborative projects, personal and action learning projects and slowly we could see improvements in building organizational consensus. Even the teams across functions could see the change. Today they are a strategic team that spends most of their time in critical thinking, faster decisions, how to solve organizational challenges without being biased on their function. So the job of HR Head is to influence collaboration across the organization and ensure it is working well.

I'm there for you:- A typical problem is when leaders start getting people Collaborate, they face a different problem: overdoing it. Too often people will try to collaborate on everything and wind up in endless meetings, debating ideas, and struggling to find consensus. They can't reach decisions and execute quickly. Effective collaborative leaders assume a strong role of director showing a path and know when to end the discussions. The Manager should show a strong hand that they are there to guide and mentor. The collaborator should be an effective leader in giving the message I'm there for you to support you to become a better leader in collaboration.

Harness Ideas:- The job of the effective collaborator is to be able to Harness ideas, people, and resources across functions. That requires reinventing their talent strategies and building strong connections both inside and outside their functions. Differences in convictions, cultural values, and operating norms inevitably add complexity to collaborative efforts. But they also make them richer, more innovative, and more valuable. Getting the value is the heart of collaborative leadership.

By then Sameer understood that while we cannot always expect people to change around us, we should horn and practice competence, behaviors which will make him successful like what I spoke above is to Build a relationship, Know your Business well and Collaborate well this three will make you a valuable contributory and member of the team.

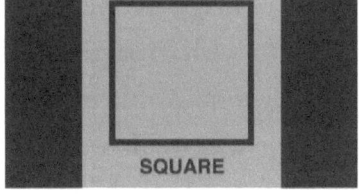

Bubble Headed Thinking   **Square Headed Thinking**

Business CHRO	Traditional HR HEAD
• Chief Change Officer • Business Lead • Talent Strategist • Build Digital Culture • Drive high performance/ enhance employee productivity • Anticipates business and talent threats and opportunities • Well versed with P&L and can contribute to growth	• Talent Manager • HR operations Manager • Functional focus • Surveyor of employee engagement • Maintain monolithic culture • Promote diversity. • Does regular HR stuff.

Business CHRO Vs Traditional HR Head

Organizations expectation is more of a Business HR then a Traditional regular HR. A Business oriented CHRO is a person who has a buddle thinking, he/she always thinks of Business growth through best people strategy, where as a traditional HR head does thinks within its boundary and limited to functional thinking. The Definition for a HR Leader is one who is a proactive HR and also manages traditional HR well. An

Average HR Manager is one who spends more time in regular HR and has little to do with Proactive HR. Today a Business CHRO is chief change officer responsible for bringing changes in the organization in leadership, the way we do our business, build a culture of productivity and high performance which is quite different from traditional HR. HR professionals has to make this transformation from Traditional HR Manager to Business HR Heads/CHRO's to align themselves with current and future business requirements.

To conclude chapter 1, It is within you to demand respect by proving your worth/capabilities. So it is a myth that HR always does what management wants them to do. Yes HR has to align with the organizational objectives/demands and plan your strategies accordingly so that you can never go wrong and if someone like the (story 1 CEO) points you out and make you uncomfortable you can always give back in a professional manner so that he understands his mistakes.

2

How Can HR Come Out of the Sandwich Position (between Employer/Management and Employee) and Perform a Clear Mindset Job Role

A Brief......

While speaking to different Industry leaders, I could get a sense that few HR Heads feel they get sandwiched sometimes and few feel it is up to the HR Head whether you want to get sandwiched or not. Many a time we have seen HR being sandwiched between employer/management and employee. Reasons may be many few are

Management sometimes may not be clear in communication to the organization about the organization's growth, future; challenges, etc and HR may not be able to answer all queries of employees. Employees may blame HR for not cascading information across the organization. An employee feels HR are there to police them and not to support

Sometimes HR is in a dilemma on how to approach a situation which has something to do with retrenchment, rationalization, termination, etc Generally, the communication flow in most cases/

organizations is a top-down approach and in that case sometimes may become a punching back from the bottom up to HR.

What makes HR come out of the sandwich situation or avoid a sandwich situation; there are few areas where HR has to have a better employee-employer relationship which can avoid sandwich situations.

Positive Conflicts - Speaks about good fights for a organizational gain. 6 tactics of positive conflicts.

What makes HR in a difficult position of being sandwiched is when we get into conflicts, many of the organizations avoid conflicts, but having a positive conflict or a good fight is rather more beneficial to organization and individual. How do I have a positive conflict to avoid sandwich situations? There was an article which I read sometimes back, which says how management/teams can have a good fight. The best teams use these six tactics to separate substantive issues from personalities.

For an HR professional it is very important to first understand the issue/Facts/concern/situation very well – Arm yourselves with a wealth of data about your business and your people. This encourages you to debate critical issues, not argue out of ignorance. We had a Senior HR leader and board member IN Orkla team, he used to always come prepared with people who is participating in the meeting, their required details, who said what in last meeting, thorough with minutes of last meeting. Pre-read and understand a bit more in depth about the discussion points, have datas ready to question/validate etc. Now because he comes so well prepared, the members of the group and presenters didn't have much choice but to equip well and come for the meeting.

```
        Facts/Data
Alternatives              Common Goals
         Theory of Having a
         Positive Conflicts
Humor                     Balance Power
        Seek Consensus
```

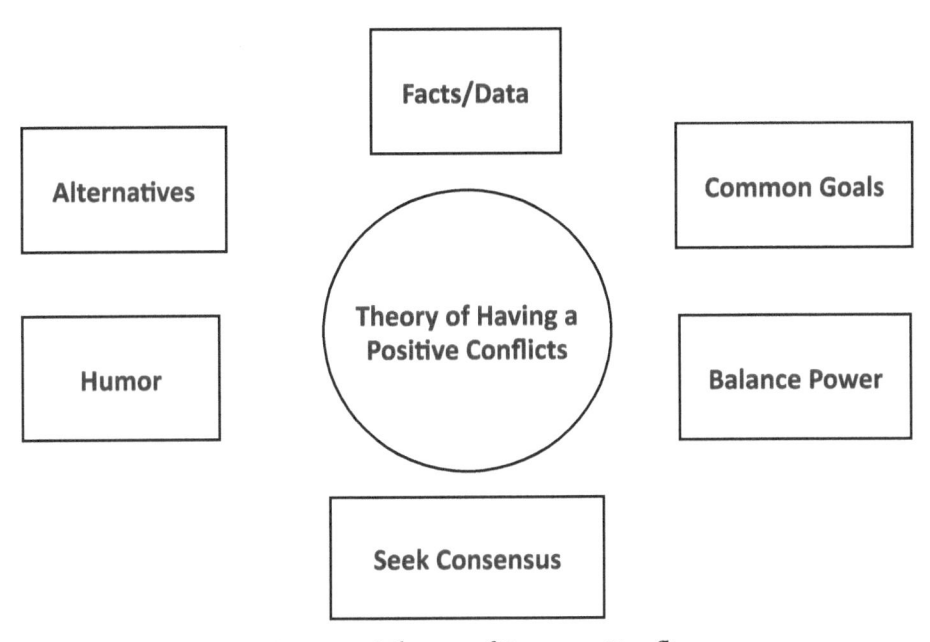

Six Tactics, Theory of Positive Conflicts

The second factor is "Look at various alternatives"– In weighing decisions, consider four or five options at once – even some you don't support. This diffuses conflicts, preventing teams from polarizing around just two possibilities.

Example- To improve the Company's performance, managers gathered facts and then brainstormed a range of alternatives, including radically redirecting strategy with entry into a new market, and even selling the company. The team combined elements of several options to arrive at a creative, robust solution.

The third factor would be how I create common objectives/goals. Unite a team with common goals. This rallies everyone to work on decisions as collaborators, making it in everyone's interest to achieve the best solution. Example – I was consulting a hospitality company defining their vision, the mission of the organization we were looking for a common theme which can inspire employee as a common goal of the organization, we named it as creating future for the hospitality industry. This company wanted to do something innovative, unique in terms of the digital platform in the hospitality industry. This was taken very well by employees and their KPI/Goals were curved based on how do they create a future for the hospitality industry.

Fourth factor - Humor plays a very important role in our lives, so using humor even if it seems contrived at times relieves tension and promotes collaborative esprit within a team. Practical jokes, Halloween and April Fool's day celebrations, and dessert "pig outs" relax everyone –increasing tactfulness, effective listening, and creativity. Let me illustrate an example for you. One of my board members (In one of the company I worked) had wonderful sense of humor, he used to crack witty jokes when situation was very serious and then everyone use to take a break and relax have a good laugh and then back to business with improvements in thoughts. Hence humor plays a very important part in corporate life.

Fifth Factor - Balance the power structure:-The CEO's is more powerful than other executives, but the others wield substantial power as well – especially in their areas of responsibility. This lets the whole team participate in strategic decisions, establishing fairness and guilty

The sixth element is to Seek consensus with qualification. If the team can't reach consensus, the most relevant senior managers make the decision guided by inputs from others. Like balancing the power structure, this tactic also builds fairness and equity. Let me give an example – One of the food company had a problem of sabotage, their products were video graphed during production and it shows some confidential information which not supposed to be known in the market for reasons of unnecessary conflicts. This video recording was brought to management by an external activist demanding donation if not will be published in the newspaper. Management understood that it was a donation demanding tactics. They looked into various options, but couldn't conclude. Then the Head HR took a decision not to entertain such people after taking stock of the entire situation and taking legal advice whatever may be the situation coming up. After a few months the issue died naturally. So it is safe, fair, and proves maturity when to seek consensus with qualification.

Fighting Teams - Developing teams that have positive fighting spirits

For HR Heads/HR Managers it important that they deal with developing teams which has positive fighting spirits this will help HR and teams to avoid getting sandwich like situation. How can HR Managers encourage the kind of substantive debate over issues that lead to better decision making? There are few approaches that help generate constructive disagreement within a team:

Heterogeneous teams – Look for diversity in teams which includes diverse ages, genders, functional background and industry experience. If everyone in the meetings sounds alike, then the chances are excellent that they probably think alike too.

How often team meets – Team members that don't know one another well don't know one another's positions on issues, impairing their ability to argue effectively. Frequent interaction builds the mutual confidence and familiarity team members require to express dissent.

Encourage team members to assume roles beyond their obvious product, geographic or functional responsibilities. Devil's advocates, sky –gazing visionaries, and action-oriented executives can work together to ensure that all sides of an issue are considered.

Apply multiple mind-sets to issue: - Try role-playing, putting yourself in your other's shoes, or conducting war games. Such techniques create fresh perspective and engage team members, spurring interest in problem solving.

Build Heterogeneous Fighting teams for the organization

Actively manage differences or conflicts:- Don't let the team acquiesce too soon or too easily. Identify and treat apathy early, and don't confuse a lack of conflicts with agreement. Often, what passes for consensus is really disengagement.

HR should diplomatically engage teams in positive and open fight so as to avoid them getting sandwiched between employee and employer.

What and How do you communicate to develop positive mindset.

HR leaders job is not to facilitate communication in the organization, but also be active ambassador and owner of all organizational communication this will avoid blame game and confusion in the organization. You must have seen many of the employees in the organization blame HR or Management when there is an improper communication or delay in communication. Mostly it is HR and then management, so effective communication plays a very vital role to eradicate sandwich kind of situations. Now the question arises how do HR communicate in a positive manner.

As you are aware a good culture defines how effectiveness is communication in the organization. Culture casts its influence over good communication through four of its important facets.

Desire Response - A quality communication brings about the desired understanding, impact and response. A message may have been received, understood and acknowledged but if not responded as expected by the sender/desirer, the communication is rendered ineffective. Evoking the desired response is the crux of effective communication. One reason for the ineffectiveness could be that what the receiver has understood of the communication may not be what the sender would have meant. Consequently, the impact or the response of the receiver would be at a variance from the sender's expectations. The other could be that thought the communication is understood. It has failed to create the desired impact on the receiver. Communication therefore is not merely the passage of a message or its expression but more importantly, the manner in which its contents have been conveyed, received and the desired response evoked from the recipient. Let me illustrate with few examples.

In one of my company I worked. I conducted an employee opinion survey for all the employees, while for all managerial staff it was in English and online survey. The survey for workmen was in the local language (the survey questions were same). They used to do paper pencil method as getting online test for workmen in local language those day was difficult. There was section on Diversity and Inclusion, which had few questions under that, our HR team couldn't explain them properly and made workers confused and when results came we show very high scores in Diversity and Inclusions and we then got to know all rated those questions under this section as 5 in scale of 1 to 5. This is actually misleading, HR team couldn't make workers understood the questions and hence the damage.

Another example I would like to describe. A well know Manufacturing organization was going through rationalization as the business was not doing so well. The company hired an external consulting company to find out reasons for not growing, how to the company grow better, cost efficiency, manpower rationalization etc. One of the major task was to relook at the organization structure and its viability in the market. When the new structure was read to roll out, just before that CEO along with his management team address the Head office staff and Factory employees on the new structure to be implemented in the organization for better decision making and faster action to customer's queries. Since Regional heads of all regions were also present, they were asked to communicate to the regional staff accordingly. This was done as the company by then had stopped all travel requests due to cost cutting. Even though all materials related to Organization structure restructuring was send to them, but they failed to communicate to regional teams in detail and effective manner. CEO being inquisitive to know how is the new structure working at regions, decided to attend Regional meetings this time. During his visit he could find employees at regions were somewhat dis-satisfied and being concerned of uncertainty. HR was asked to conduct a study/survey at regions and they finally found that the expectations of the employees on rationalization and what the regional head had communicated are different and hence employees at regions lost confidence on management and HR. While things were sorted out in few days. But the initial damage which was done cannot be revived. This is a typical example of how communication can fail if not communicated in manner which is understood and digested by employees.

Effectiveness and Efficiency: Communication should be effective and efficient. In certain situations, the most efficient method may not necessarily be the most effective. When the two conflicts, priority has obviously to be for the effective mode. For example, putting up an important and urgent communication on the notice board for those working on a shop floor may be the most efficient way of communication but may not be the most effective too, especially if the message requires some explanation, or if the reaction time is short and people may not get to see the notice board in time. Other less efficient but more effective modes like personal contact, public address system, addressing by name etc. may be required to make that communication serve its purpose effectively under those circumstances. Efficiency should serve effectiveness.

When I was in 5th grade schooling, one day I got hurt on head while doing a stunt in school impressing class fellows. Like many other kids I was one of the naughty type always looking for new pranks and naughty ideas. My 3rd sister who was elder than me called my Dad at his office on telephone as there were no mobile phones in 1986. My sister was very talkative and used to exaggerate things a bit always not as intentional but that is how she was. With lot of difficulty in getting telephone line connection my sister could convey the message that I was hurt in the head and leg badly, but due to bad connection he heard as my head has a crack and leg broke badly and he is needed to rush to hospital as early as possible. My Dad started immediately from office to reach house, with full panic and what to do thought? he was also accompanied by his friend and colleague. While coming together he was discussing with his friend which hospital was good for admitting me and what measures should be taken. Once he reached home he could find me fine and I have a small crack on my head which was treaded by a local doctor. He could breathe with relief after seeing me and knowing what happened to me. See how an improper/incomplete communication can put people in trouble and make them tense.

Second incidence, in one of my company I worked we had an annual conference in Goa. While we were all busy with conference we did have time for recreational activities. Entire Managerial level employees were present in the conference. Our IT Head a good talker but a nice person was also present in the conference. He had a habit of boosting himself by talking about himself. At an evening dinner during one of the conference days, he told us (15-20 Managers) that he was a national swimmer and have won many medals, he can bit anyone in swimming. We all were very impressed that we have a national swimmer in our company. Next day we all went for swimming in the Hotel pool. he got into pool with lot of enthusiasm and we all were eager to see his swift swimming. But in sometime we saw him sinking and sinking with his hand up. We though he is showing us some trick. To our surprise we realized he need help and was getting drowned. One of our Managers jumped into the pool and saved him. He later said he was not swimming for many years. Now the point here is why he tried to impress people and mis-communicate his ability when he had not been swimming for many years and now he wanted to show few stunts. We all were thinking he was a great swimmer and that is the reason we didn't go to rescue him initially as he was trying performing few stunts. So it is very important what you communicate and based on which the expectations are build up.

What you have:- The content is very important in any communication whether it is a text or verbal. In text communication, especially the language in which a communication is phrased and communicated, is vital for its effectiveness. Semantics plays an important role in conveying the text in its intended perspective and meaning. These should be in keeping with the intelligence, language proficiency, contextual perspective and the knowledge of the receiver. This aspect gets all the more crucial when the communication system is serving people from diverse cultural, educational and social backgrounds.

Those expressions which are liable for multiple interpretations should be avoided. It should always be kept in mind that the communication is intended for the receiver to comprehend with the same perspective which the sender had intended. If the text is beyond the comprehension of the receiver, the message is as good as not received. In case it is misunderstood or misinterpreted. The consequences could be worse than if the communication had not been made at all. In spite of the availability of an efficient channel such a communication would be ineffective.

A typical example which organizations face is the Performance related communication. R&D and Innovation function plays a very important role in FMCG organization. There was a R&D head who was reporting to VP Operations. The VP operations were a very shrewd personality with high on task and low on people management, He was not so happy with the performance of the R&D Head. So he tried communicating orally to him but not hitting the actual issue but giving him a overall view on this performance. End of the session the R&D Head used to always be confused whether he has told good about this performance or bad. Neither had he used to give anything in writing about this performance except few words in his appraisal to close the PMS process which never had anything to say about his performance in detail his areas of improvement and what timelines he wanted to give him to improve. After few months the VP got very much annoyed with his performance and called him and said you are fired. The R&D Head took this as a shock as he was never expecting his boss to directly fire him without giving any proper feedback or development/improvement plan. The R&D Head came up to the HR Head and complained that how can VP Ops ask him to leave without proper written feedback on performance over the year. He was right on his part. The HR Head spoke to VP operations and he said that he had already indicated in appraisal, but HR Head said you never mentioned anything bad on his performance appraisal, only few development plans and his rating. Of course things were handled in different way later but have u seen how confusing it can be if you don't communicate in writing properly and then explain the receiver. It may turn worse, doesn't matter whether it is official or personal.

Who is at Other end:- As a HR professionals you should always be aware and analyze who is your possible target audience. Infact detail out the list of groups, members, levels etc and then start preparing your communication pack based on the maturity levels and impact of the communication. Also there is no point in communicating when there is no one to respond at the other end. It would be like talking to wilderness with no one around to listen. It may so happen that while one is sending a message, the receiver at the other end is either not mentally or emotionally tuned to receive the communication: or may be just hearing but not listening. The effect would still be similar to talking to wilderness.

An well know organization once was launching its Vision Mission and Values(VMV) of the organization. They had hired an consultant who ran the entire workshop and then finalize the VMV of the organization with top 50 Managers of the organization. A big launch was made and was cascaded across organization with CEO's and CXO's speech. HO, Factories, regional offices etc was taken through the entire package of VMV. It was difficult for entire regional team to travel to corporate office, hence was conveyed thorough webinar. Everything went on well the company decided to go ahead and implement the same. After a month CEO and his Direct reports travelled to regions on review. The CEO asked one of the employees about VMV implementation, none of them could say things properly as they were not fully aware of VMV roll out. Some who attend the lecture either didn't understand the whole VMV thing or ever got interested to ask more about VMV as it has no direct impact with salaries or sales targets. CEO was very disappointed and informed HR head to roll out the VMV session personally at all regions and branches and make them understand what it means to the organization and them. So analyzing target audience and planning communication pack is very important.

Another example which is quite commonly happens in the organization when it comes to termination of an employee. The HR Head of a manufacturing company took a service termination letter to his CEO for his signature. The CEO was explained that the employees had been absent for long without any communication form him for grant of leave. The mandatory letters sent by registered post, too had not brought any response. After consulting legal advisor and as per company rules, the HR Head came to a conclusion that he has to be fired.

The CEO was not convinced first of all because this employee didn't have any records of continuous absenteeism and was a decent worker. He wanted to know if someone tried reaching him. The HR Head said there was no response from his phone as well. The CEO before signing wanted to make sure we have tried all options of reaching him. He wasn't taking the easier line of action. He asked HR head to send someone to his house and try finding out the facts. HR Head along with his Employee relations Manager went to this workmen's house. After reaching this workmen's house they were surprised to see he was in miserable condition suffering from a bout of malaria with a few days old baby. His wife died during delivery and he was looking after the infant, sick himself and without any help. He couldn't even recharge his phone as he couldn't move out of his house, hence switched off the phone. He was expecting his mother to fetch up from the distant village to enable him to re-join duty. Instead of terminating the services, both the worker and the baby, were promptly moved to a nursing home. The HR Head had dutifully transmitted the message to the employee but in reality communicated with no one whereas the CEO has communicated. We can be sure that the HR Head had learnt an important lesson in communication on the emotional plane that day. A sender has to ensure that his message had been listened to effectively by those for whom it is intended.

Communication through Grapevine channels:- As HR head you have to keep your ears and eyes open for such communication. While Grapevine communication may cause damage to organization reputation and culture, but it has also been proven that Grapevine communication indirect helps organizations to communicate not so good news, like restructuring, retrenchments etc. Its existence and usage reflects the basic need of the people to know what is going on in and around the areas of their interests and the instinctive urge to pass on that information to others. Whatever be the degree of effectiveness of the usual communications, the grapevine would always exist. However in the absence of transparency and effectiveness in the top down communication, this mode of communication becomes highly potent. It has the inherent dubious characteristics of becoming a source for generation of rumors and a ready channel for their circulation which snowball as they spread. Grapevine loses its appeal and circulation where the organization channels are transparent and the leadership takes care to use them to keep the people informed. As mentioned above many HR leaders use this communication tactics effectively to get mixed information from the employees. This helps HR to analyze the outcome and prepare better communication plan with less chances of suppresses, confusions or errors.

One of the organizations was going through a major revamp due to business volatility in the market. They thought of hiring a consultant for restructuring the organization structure based on new Vision, mission of the company and Business priorities. While this consultant was doing his job with the HR team which went for a month or so, there were rumors floating in the organization that organization is going to retrench employees, few may be demoted and many may ask to leave the organization. The Grapevine communication was so strong that it almost sounded like real news, in fact that gave them ideas to communicate in a manner which was understood by employees. The HR dept could analyze where the pain areas are and where they can stretch a bit. Infact few who were not performing that well in the organization had a preconceived notion that they may be asked to quit the organization, hence kind of mentally prepared.

As HR being the custodian of communication in the organization they should listen more often than any function in the organization rather spending time in communicating to employees. The HR head should focus on these questions to ensure effective communication both in upwards, downwards, lateral communication and external communication.

What kind of communication system you have got? What is the degree of centralization of communication channels? Does it allow for easy accessibility of the channels to all those who need to use them?

HR head to analyze what is the actual flow of the traffic through the channels? A special note should be taken of the traffic through the upward communication channels

How the norms of effective listening are observed by the team members especially its leader? It has special relevance to discussions during the meetings.

Does the culture lay emphasis on effective communication visa-a-vis efficient means.

What is the general frequency of holding meetings? Is it too frequent or too less?

Are meetings marked by free and frank raising of issues and discussions?

What is the standard of preparatory effort made for meetings, especially that of preparation of agenda? What is the general reaction of the members to the effectiveness of the meetings?

What is the system of follow-up action on the minutes of meetings?

How can HR Heads develop the Art of persuasion

It is kind of mandatory for HR heads to develop the art of persuasion. It is not only about communicating well but how the communication does makes an impact to the target audience. This is True about any Managers and Leaders. If there ever was a time for business people to learn the fine art of persuasion, it is now. Gone are the command-and-control days of executives managing by decree. Today businesses are run largely by cross-functional teams of peers and populated by baby boomers and their generations X offspring, who show little tolerance for unquestioned authority. Electronic communication and globalization have further eroded the traditional hierarchy, as ideas and people flow more freely than ever around organizations and as decisions get made closer to the markets. These fundamental changes, more than a decade in the making but now firmly part of the economic landscape, essentially come down to this: work today gets done in an environment where people don't just ask What should I do? but Why should I do it?

To answer this why question effectively is to persuade. Yet many business people misunderstand persuasion, and more still underutilize it. The reason? Persuasion is widely perceived as a skill reserved for selling products and closing deals. It is also commonly seen as just another form of manipulation-devious and to be avoided. Certainly persuasion can be used in selling and deal-clinching situations, and it can be misused to manipulate people. But exercised constructively and to its full potential, persuasion supersedes sales and is quite the opposite of deception. Effective persuasion becomes a negotiating and learning process through which a persuader leads colleagues to a problem's shared solution. Persuasion does indeed involve moving people to a position they don't currently hold, but not by begging or cajoling. Instead, it involves careful preparation, the proper framing of arguments, the presentation of vivid supporting evidence, and the effort to find the correct emotional match with your audience.

Effective persuasion is a difficult and time consuming proposition, but it may also be more powerful than the command-and-control managerial model it succeeds. As Allied Signal's CEO Lawrence Bossily said sometime back "The day when you could yell and scream and beat people into good performance is over. Today you have to appeal to them by helping them see how they can get from here to there, by establishing some credibility, and giving them some reasons and help them to get there. Do all those things, and they will knock down doors" In essence, he is describing persuasion- now more than ever, the language of business leadership.

Persuasion is relatively a straight forward process. First, you strongly state your position. Second, you outline the supporting arguments, followed by a highly assertive, data-based exposition. Finally, you enter the deal-making stage and work towards a "close". In the other words, you use logic, persistence, and personal enthusiasm to get others to buy a good idea. The reality is that following this process is one surefire way to fail at persuasion.

Why persuasion fails

In Organizations I worked and as a consultant I have seen many Managers fail miserably at persuasion. They make common mistakes

1. They attempt to make their case with an up-front, hard sell. Managers strongly state their position at the outset, and then through a process of persistence, logic, and exuberance, they try to push the idea to a close. In reality, setting out a strong position at the start of a persua- sion effort gives potential opponents something to grab onto – and fight against. It's far better to present your position with the finesse and reserve of a lion tamer, who engages his "partner" by showing him the legs of a chair. In other words, effective persuaders don't begin the process by giving their colleagues a clear target in which to set their jaws.

2. They resist compromise. Too many managers see compromise as surrender, but it is essential to constructive persuasion. Before people buy into a proposal, they want to see that the persuader is flexible enough to respond to their concerns. Compromises can often lead to better, more sustainable shared solutions. By not compromising, ineffective persuaders un- consciously send the message that they think persuasion is a one-way street. But persuasion is a process of give-and-take. Kathleen Reardon, a professor of organizational behavior at the University of Southern California, points out that a persuader rarely changes another person's behavior or viewpoint without altering his or her own in the process. To persuade meaning- fully, we must not

only listen to others but also incorporate their perspectives into our own.
3. They think the secret of persuasion lies in presenting great arguments. In persuading people to change their minds, great arguments matter. No doubt about it. But arguments, per se, are only one part of the equation. Other factors matter just as much, such as the persuader's credibility and his or her ability to create a proper, mutually beneficial frame for a position, connect on the right emotional level with an audience, and communicate through vivid language that makes arguments come alive.
4. They assume persuasion is a one-shot effort. Persuasion is a process, not an event. Rarely, if ever, is it possible to arrive at a shared solution on the first try. More often than not, persuasion involves listening to people, testing a position, developing a new position that reflects input from the group, more testing, incorporating compromises, and then trying again. If this sounds like a slow and difficult process, that's because it is. But the results are worth the effort.

In one of my company where I worked we had a sales head, Chief Sales Officer, He was quite an experienced employee with good sales management skills. But he always came across as an aggressive presenter, may be because of his long experience in field sales. He was very confident in his approach and used to think his solutions is the best. He had a mind-set that his proposal cannot be disputed and hardly has any flaws. He would argue and argue to make his point win, without understanding what other used to say in meetings. It so happened that he was being ignored by his peers and other cross functional members. My MD and me had few sessions with him to make him understand where he goes wrong and why should be become better in persuasion rather demanding consensus from management group. For few days he used to be behaving better, then after some days he was back to his original behaviour.

If persuasion is learning and negotiating process, then in the most general terms it involves phases of discovery, preparation, and dialogue. Getting ready to persuade colleagues can take weeks or months of planning as you learn about your audience and the position you intend to argue. Before they even start to talk, effective persuaders have considered their positions from every angle. What investments in time and money will my position require from others? Is my supporting evidence weak in any way? Are there alternative positions I need to examine? Dialogue happens before and during the persuasion process. Before the process begins, effective persuaders use dialogue to learn more about their audience's opinions, concerns, and perspectives. During the process, dialogue continues to be a form of learning, but it is also the beginning of the negotiation stage. You invite people to discuss, even debate, the merits of your position, and then to offer honest feedback and suggest alternative solutions. That may sound like a slow way to achieve your goal, but effective persuasion is about testing and revising ideas in concert with your colleagues' concerns and needs. In fact, the best persuaders not only listen to others but also incorporate their perspective into a shared solution.

Persuasion, in other words, often involves – indeed, demands – compromise. Perhaps that is why the most effective persuaders seem to share a common trait: they are open-minded, never dogmatic. They enter the persuasion process prepared to adjust their viewpoints and incorporate others' ideas. That approach to persuasion is, interestingly, highly persuasive in itself. When colleagues see that a persuader is eager to hear their views and willing to make changes in response to their needs and concerns, they respond very positively. They trust the persuader more and listen more attentively. They don't fear being bowled over or manip- ulated. They see the persuader as flexible and are thus more willing to make sacrifices themselves. Because that is such a powerful dynamic, good persuaders often enter the persuasion process with judicious compromises already prepared.

For your to be a good persuader/influencer you have to First define your audience. Are you trying to influence a specific group of people, such as your employee group? Or are you trying to influence a larger target audience, such as Twitter followers or bloggers? Are you trying to influence potential clients or customers? Or are you trying to influence the field of Human Resources as a business and psychological sphere? These are questions you need to think about. The good news is that regardless of the answer there are some commonalities.

Effective persuasion involves Four distinct and essential steps. First, effective persuaders establish credibility. Second, they frame their goals in a way that identifies common ground with those they in- tend to persuade. Third, they reinforce their positions using vivid language and compelling evidence. And fourth, they connect emotionally with their audience. As one of the most effective executives in our research commented, "The most valuable lesson I've learned about persuasion over the years is that there's just as much strategy in how you present your position as in the position itself. In fact, I'd say the strategy of presentation is the more critical."

Build credibility

The first hurdle persuaders must overcome is their own credibility. A persuader can't advocate a new or contrarian position without having people wonder, Can we trust this individual's perspectives and opinions? Such a reaction is understandable. After all, allowing oneself to be persuaded is risky, because any new initiative demands a commitment of time and resources. Yet even though persuaders must have high credibility, our research strongly suggests that most managers overestimate their own credibility – considerably. In the workplace, credibility grows out of two sources: expertise and relationships. People are considered to have high levels of expertise if they have a history of sound judgment or have proven themselves knowledgeable and well informed about their proposals. For example, in proposing a new product idea, an effective persuader would need to be perceived as possessing a thorough understanding of the product – its specifications, target markets, customers, and competing products. A history of prior successes would further strengthen the per- suader's perceived expertise. One extremely successful executive in our research had a track record of 14 years of devising highly effective advertising campaigns. Not surprisingly, he had an easy time winning colleagues over to his position. Another manager had a track record of seven successful new-product launches in a period of five years. He, too, had an advantage when it came to persuading his colleagues to support his next new idea.

On the relationship side, people with high credibility have demonstrated – again, usually over time – that they can be trusted to listen and to work in the best interests of others. They have also consistently shown strong emotional character and integrity; that is, they are not known for mood extremes or inconsistent performance. Indeed, people who are known to be honest, steady, and reliable have an edge when going into any persuasion situation. Because their relationships are robust, they are more apt to be given the benefit of the doubt. One effective persuader in our research was considered by colleagues to be remarkably trustworthy and fair; many people confided in her. In addition, she generously shared credit for good ideas and pro- vided staff with exposure to the company's senior executives. This woman had built strong relation- ships, which meant her staff and peers were always willing to consider seriously what she proposed. If expertise and relationships determine credibility, it is crucial that you undertake an honest assessment of where you stand on both criteria before beginning to persuade. To do so, first step back and ask yourself the following questions related to expertise: How will others perceive my knowledge about the strategy, product, or change I am proposing? Do I have a track record in this area that others know about and respect? Then, to assess the strength of your relationship credibility, ask your- self, Do those I am hoping to persuade see me as helpful, trustworthy, and supportive? Will they see me as someone in sync with them – emotionally, intellectually, and politically – on issues like this one? Finally, it is important to note that it is not enough to get your own read on these matters. You must also test your answers with colleagues you trust to give you a reality check. Only then will you have a complete picture of your credibility. In most cases, that exercise helps people discover that they have some measure of weakness, either on the expertise or on the relationship side of credibility. The challenge then becomes to fill in such gaps. In general if your area of weakness is on the experts side then you have several options:

First, you can learn more about the complexities of your position through either formal or informal education and through conversations with knowl- edgeable individuals. You might also get more relevant experience on the job by asking, for instance, to be assigned to a team that would increase your insight into particular markets or products.

Another alternative is to hire someone to bolster your expertise – for example, an industry consultant or a recognized outside expert, such as a professor. Either one may have the knowledge and experience required to support your position effectively. Similarly, you may tap experts within your organization to advocate your position. Their credibility becomes a substitute for your own

You can also utilize other outside sources of information to support your position, such as respected business or trade periodicals, books, independently produced reports, and lectures by experts. In our research, one executive from the clothing industry successfully persuaded his company to reposition an entire product line to a more youthful market after bolstering his credibility with articles by a noted demographer in two highly regarded journals and with two independent market-research studies.

Finally, you may launch pilot projects to demonstrate on a small scale your expertise and the value of your ideas.

As for filling in the relationship gap: You should make a concerted effort to meet one- on-one with all the key people you plan to persuade. This is not the time to outline your position but rather to get a range of perspectives on the issue at hand. If you have the time and resources, you should even offer to help these people with issues that concern them.

Another option is to involve like-minded co-workers who already have strong relationships with your audience. Again, that is a matter of seeking out substitutes on your own behalf.

For an example of how these strategies can be put to work, consider the case of a Chief operating officer of a large retail bank, whom we will call Tom Smith. Although he was new to his job, Smith ardently wanted to persuade the senior management team that the company was in serious trouble. He believed that the bank's overhead was excessive and would jeopardize its position as the industry entered a more competitive era. Most of his col- leagues, however, did not see the potential serious- ness of the situation. Because the bank had been enormously successful in recent years, they believed changes in the industry posed little danger. In addition to being newly appointed, Smith had another problem: his career had been in financial services, and he was considered an outsider in the world of retail banking. Thus he had few personal connections to draw on as he made his case, nor was he perceived to be particularly knowledgeable about marketplace exigencies.

As a first step in establishing credibility, Smith hired an external consultant with respected credentials in the industry who showed that the bank was indeed poorly positioned to be a low-cost producer. In a series of interactive presentations to the bank's top-level management, the consultant revealed how the company's leading competitors were taking aggressive actions to contain operating costs. He made it clear from these presentations that not cutting costs would soon cause the bank to fall drastically behind the competition. These findings were then distributed in written reports that circulated throughout the bank

Next, Smith determined that the bank's branch managers were critical to his campaign. The buy-in of those respected and informed individuals would signal to others in the company that his concerns were valid. Moreover, Smith looked to the branch managers because he believed that they could in- crease his expertise about marketplace trends and also help him test his own assumptions. Thus, for the next three months, he visited every branch in his region of Ontario, Canada – 135 in all. During each visit, he spent time with branch managers, lis- tening to their perceptions of the bank's strengths and weaknesses. He learned firsthand about the competition's initiatives and customer trends, and he solicited ideas for improving the bank's services and minimizing costs. By the time he was through, Smith had a broad perspective on the bank's future that few people even in senior management possessed. And he had built dozens of relationships in the process

Finally, Smith launched some small but highly visible initiatives to demonstrate his expertise and capabilities. For example, he was concerned about slow growth in the company's mortgage business and the loan officers' resulting slip in morale. So he devised a program in which new mortgage customers would make no payments for the first 90 days. The initiative proved remarkably successful, and in short order Smith appeared to be a far more savvy retail banker than anyone had assumed.

Another example of how to establish credibility comes from Microsoft. In 1990, two product-development managers, Karen Fries and Barry Linnett, came to believe that the market would greatly welcome software that featured a "social interface." They envisioned a package that would employ animated human and animal characters to show users how to go about their computing tasks. Inside Microsoft, however, employees had immediate concerns about the concept. Software programmers ridiculed the cute characters. Animated characters had been used before only in software for children, making their use in adult environments hard to envision. But Fries and Linnett felt their proposed product had both dynamism and complexity, and they remained convinced that consumers would eagerly buy such programs. They also believed that the home-computer software market – largely untapped at the time and with fewer software standards – would be open to such innovation.

Within the company, Fries had gained quite a bit of relationship credibility. She had started out as a recruiter for the company in 1987 and had worked directly for many of Microsoft's senior executives. They trusted and liked her. In addition, she had been responsible for hiring the company's product and program managers. As a result, she knew all the senior people at Microsoft and had hired many of the people who would be deciding on her product. Linnett's strength laid in his expertise. In particular, he knew the technology behind an innovative tutorial program called PC Works. In addition, both Fries and Linnett had managed Publisher, a product with a unique help feature called Wizards, which Microsoft's CEO, Bill Gates, had liked. But those factors were sufficient only to get an initial hearing from Microsoft's senior management. To persuade the organization to move forward, the pair would need to improve perceptions of their expertise. It hurt them that this type of social-interface software had no proven track record of success and that they were both novices with such software. Their challenge became one of finding substitutes for their own expertise.

Their first step was a wise one. From within Microsoft, they hired respected technical guru Darrin Massena. With Massena, they developed a set of prototypes to demonstrate that they did indeed understand the software's technology and could make it work. They then tested the prototypes in market research, and users responded enthusiastically. Finally, and most important, they enlisted two Stan- ford University professors, Clifford Nass and Bryon Reeves, both experts in human-computer interaction. In several meetings with Microsoft senior managers and Gates himself, they presented a rigorously compiled and thorough body of research that demonstrated how and why social-interface software was ideally suited to the average computer user. In addition, Fries and Linnett asserted that considerable jumps in computing power would make more realistic cartoon characters an increasingly malleable technology. Their products, they said, was the leading edge of an incipient software revolution. Convinced, Gates approved a full product- development team, and in January 1995, the product called BOB was launched. BOB went on to sell more than half a million copies, and its concept and technology are being used within Microsoft as a platform for developing several Internet products. Credibility is the cornerstone of effective persuading; without it, a persuader won't be given the time of day. In the best-case scenario, people enter into a persuasion situation with some measure of expertise and relationship credibility. But it is important to note that credibility along either line can be built or bought. Indeed, it must be, or the next steps are an exercise in futility.

Let me give my own experience example. As a HR Head of a well-known FMCG MNC one of my key responsibilities was to build culture of digitization in the organization. We formed a steering committee comprising of Board members, CEO, External IT consultants and our CFO as IT was under his responsibility. Functional CXO's were responsible for their respective functions digitization. I was responsible to bring best of HR Digitization system which can replace the existing system. The management was not so keen on HR digitization and had priority set after sales, operations, supply chain and finance function. But it was important for us to change the existing system as it was obsoleted and upgrading that would cost us a huge amount of money and still wouldn't give the full solution for our organization. The first step was to understand the latest technology available in market. We did enough research to find out a suitable system which quenches the need of the organization from all functions. We had challenges to find a system which can help sales function where employees work remotely from Pan India branches, Operations team where we have manufacturing plants that deals with shifts, attendance, roasters, compliances etc. And other support functions. We spend time with functions to understand the complexities and solutions expected to solve the challenges. IT and HR worked hard to understand detail technicality of the system, went through many trails and once we were confident enough we presented to the Steering committee along with our other functional heads. There was enough debate on assuring whether this is the right product for us and do we want company to consider as one of the priority. But because of Technical knowledge, analysis done on each and every functional requirement and solutions HRIS can provide and long term applications of the software/system build a lot of credibility which helped us to sail through and finally implement. So HR Folks should always have enough data to build credibility which can influence stake holders to decide better.

Frame for common ground

Even if your credibility is high, your position must still appeal strongly to the people you are trying to persuade. After all, few people will jump on board a train that will bring them to ruin or even mild discomfort. Effective persuaders must be adept at describing their positions in terms that illuminate their ad- vantages. As any parent can tell you, the fastest way to get a child to come along willingly on a trip to the grocery store is to point out that there are lollipops by the cash register. That is not deception. It is just a persuasive way of framing the benefits of taking such a journey. In work situations, persuasive framing is obviously more complex, but the underlying principle is the same. It is a process of identifying shared benefits.

Monica Ruffo, an account executive for an advertising agency, offers a good example of persuasive framing. Her client, a fast-food chain, was instituting a promotional campaign in Canada; menu items such as a hamburger, fries, and cola were to be bundled together and sold at a low price. The strategy made sense to corporate headquarters. Its research showed that consumers thought the company's products were higher priced than the competition's, and the company was anxious to overcome this perception. The franchisees, on the other hand, were still experiencing strong sales and were far more concerned about the short-term impact that the new, low prices would have on their profit margins.

A less experienced persuader would have attempted to rationalize head quarters' perspective to the franchisees – to convince them of its validity. But Ruffo framed the change in pricing to demonstrate its benefits to the franchisees themselves. The new value campaign, she explained, would actually improve franchisees' profits. To back up this point, she drew on several sources. A pilot project in Tennessee, for instance, had demonstrated that under the new pricing scheme, the sales of french fries and drinks – the two most profitable items on the menu – had markedly in- creased. In addition, the company had rolled out medium-sized meal packages in 80% of its U.S. outlets, and fran- chisees' sales of fries and drinks had jumped 26%. Citing research from a respected business periodical, Ruffo also showed that when customers raised their estimate of the value they receive from a retail establishment by 10%, the establishment's sales rose by 1%. She had estimated that the new meal plan would increase value perceptions by 100%, with the result that franchisee sales could be expected to grow 10%.

Ruffo closed her presentation with a letter written many years before by the company's founder to the organization. It was an emotional letter extolling the values of the company and stressing the importance of the franchisees to the company's success. It also highlighted the importance of the company's position as the low-price leader in the industry. The beliefs and values contained in the letter had long been etched in the minds of Ruffo's audience. Hearing them again only confirmed the company's con- cern for the franchisees and the importance of their winning formula. They also won Ruffo a standing ovation. That day, the franchisees voted unani- mously to support the new meal-pricing plan.

The Ruffo case illustrates why – in choosing appropriate positioning – it is critical first to identify your objective's tangible benefits to the people you are trying to persuade. Sometimes that is easy. Mutual benefits exist. In other situations, however, no shared advantages are readily apparent – or meaningful. In these cases, effective persuaders adjust their positions. They know it is impossible to en gage people and gain commitment to ideas or plans without highlighting the advantages to all the par- ties involved.

At the heart of framing is a solid understanding of your audience. Even before starting to persuade, the best persuaders we have encountered closely study the issues that matter to their colleagues. They use conversations, meetings, and other forms of dialogue to collect essential information. They are good at listening. They test their ideas with trusted confidants, and they ask questions of the people they will later be persuading. Those steps help them think through the arguments, the evidence, and the perspectives they will present. Oftentimes, this process causes them to alter or compromise their own plans before they even start persuading. It is through this thoughtful, inquisitive approach they develop frames that appeal to their audience. Consider the case of a manager who was in charge of process engineering for a jet engine manufacturer. He had redesigned the work flow for routine turbine maintenance for airline clients in a manner that would dramatically shorten the turnaround time for servicing. Before presenting his ideas to the company's president, he consulted a good friend in the company, the vice president of engineering, who knew the president well. This conversation revealed that the president's prime concern would not be speed or efficiency but profitability. To get the president's buy-in, the vice president explained, the new system would have to improve the com- pany's profitability in the short run by lowering operating expenses.

At first this information had the manager stumped. He had planned to focus on efficiency and had even intended to request additional funding to make the process work. But his conversation with the vice president sparked him to change his position. Indeed, he went so far as to change the work- flow design itself so that it no longer required new investment but rather drove down costs. He then carefully documented the cost savings and profitability gains that his new plan would produce and presented this revised plan to the president. With his initiative positioned anew, the manager persuaded the president and got the project approved.

My experience says that in any organization when you are trying to convenience the stake holders or functional heads/CXO's you will always be asked a question what is in for me, in the sense how does this proposal benefit my function and organization. Like in the above HRIS example I have mentioned that there were debate of many rounds and many days, because HR was trying to show case the apt benefits to functions. Convincing all and getting consensus is not a simple job. You have continuously think what best benefits you can offer to the functions.

Provide evidence

With credibility established and a common frame identified, persuasion be- comes a matter of presenting evidence. Ordinary evidence, however, won't do. We have found that the most effective persuaders use language in a particular way. They supplement numerical data with examples, stories, metaphors, and analogies to make their positions come alive. That use of language paints a vivid word picture and, in doing so, lends a compelling and tangible quality to the persuader's point of view.

Think about a typical persuasion situation. The persuader is often advocating a goal, strategy, or initiative with an uncertain outcome. Karen Fries and Barry Linnett, for instance, wanted Microsoft to invest millions of dollars in a software package with chancy technology and unknown market demand. The team could have supported its case solely with market research, financial projections, and the like. But that would have been a mistake, because research shows that most people perceive such reports as not entirely informative. They are too abstract to be completely meaningful or memorable. In essence, the numbers don't make an emotional impact.

By contrast, stories and vivid language do, particularly when they present comparable situations to the one under discussion. A marketing man- ager trying to persuade senior executives to invest in a new product, for example might cite examples of similar investments that paid off handsomely. Indeed, we found that people readily draw lessons from such cases. More important, the research shows that listeners absorb information in proportion to its vividness. Thus it is no wonder that Fries and Linnett hit a home run when they presented their case for BOB with the following analogy:

Imagine you want to cook dinner and you must first go to the supermarket. You have all the flexibility you want – you can cook anything in the world as long as you know how and have the time and desire to do it. When you arrive at the supermarket, you find all these overstuffed aisles with cryptic single-word headings like "sundries" and "ethnic food" and "condiments." These are the menus on typical computer interfaces. The question is whether salt is under condiments or ethnic food or near the potato chip section. There are surrounding racks and wall spaces, much as our software interfaces now have support buttons, tool bars, and lines around the perimeters. Now after you have collected everything, you still need to put it all together in the correct order to make a meal. If you're a good cook, your meal will probably be good. If you're a novice, it probably won't be.

Microsoft have been selling under the super- market category for years, and they think there is a big opportunity for restaurants. That's what we are trying to do now with BOB: pushing the next step with software that is more like going to a restaurant, so the user doesn't spend all of his time searching for the ingredients. We find and put the ingredients together. You sit down, you get comfortable. We bring you a menu. We do the work, you relax. It's an enjoyable experience. No walking around lost trying to find things, no cooking.

Had Fries and Linnett used a literal description of BOB's advantages, few of their highly computer literate colleagues at Microsoft would have person- ally related to the menu-searching frustration that BOB was designed to eliminate. The analogy they selected, however, made BOB's purpose both concrete and memorable.

A master persuader, Mary Kay Ash, the founder of Mary Kay Cosmetics, regularly draws on analogies to illustrate and "sell" the business conduct she values. Consider this speech at the company's annual sales convention:

Back in the days of the Roman Empire, the legions of the emperor conquered the known world. There was, however, one band of people that the Romans never conquered. Those people were the followers of the great teacher from Bethlehem. Historians have long since dis- covered that one of the reasons for the sturdiness of this folk was their habit of meeting together weekly. They shared their difficulties, and they stood side by side. Does this remind you of something? The way we stand side by side and share our knowledge and difficulties with each other in our weekly unit meetings? I have so often observed when a director or unit member is confronted with a personal problem that the unit stands together in helping that sister in distress. What a wonderful circle of friendships we have. Perhaps it's one of the greatest fringe benefits of our company.

Through her vivid analogy, Ash links collective support in the company to a courageous period in Christian history. In doing so, she accomplishes several objectives. First, she drives home her belief that collective support is crucial to the success of the organization. Most Mary Kay salespeople are independent operators who face the daily challenges of direct selling. An emotional support sys- tem of fellow salespeople is essential to ensure that self-esteem and confidence remain intact in the face of rejection. Next she suggests by her analogy that solidarity against the odds is the best way to stymie powerful oppressors to wit, the competition. Finally, Ash's choice of analogy imbues a sense of a heroic mission to the work of her sales force. You probably don't need to invoke the analogy of the Christian struggle to support your position, but effective persuaders are not afraid of unleashing the immense power of language. In fact, they use it to their utmost advantage.

Another example to quote on providing evidences to justify better results. One of the highly unionized labour intensive manufacturing companies which I worked was thinking of implementing Voluntary retirement scheme (VRS) for blue collared employees. The reason being aged workforce, low productivity and high labour cost. A team of HR, Operations and Finance was formed under my leadership to design and implement the scheme. In order to maintain confidentiality before the VRS scheme is implemented we named it as Project Fly. The team worked hard to put up all possible parameters like

- Why Project fly?
- Over View of the Scheme
- Advantages of doing in one go
- Position and people evaluation
- Backup plan
- Liability pre and post
- Timescale
- Present IR scenario

- Concerns for implementing in present scenario
- Cost analysis

This was well presented to board. While the company Board of Directors got convinced by the scheme after few presentations. But they were not yet convinced whether VRS was right method to reduce people and the reasons of implementing the same then. So we tried convincing the board on the following factors Excesses Manpower identified through productivity study, Manual work to automation hence require less manpower, Education level is very low, barriers in upgrading their skills, Efficient utilization of manpower and flexible working across units through improved manning planning, Obsolescence's of Products etc. But the board was convinced only when they saw that majority of Blue collared employees were opting for financial assistance scheme as they were aware that they could not upgrade themselves to new learning due to automation. They expected a package from the Organization which they can take and resign from the organization. This data was presented to Board and finally Board got convinced as this was a scheme in a way initiated by Blue collared employees itself other than companies' objectives. So putting up evidences which the audience (Person/Team you are going to convince) would like to know or understand is the key as a potential evidence.

Connect emotionally

In the business world, we like to think that our colleagues use reason to make their decisions, yet if we scratch below the surface we will always find emotions at play. Good persuaders are aware of the primacy of emotions and are responsive to them in two important ways.

First, they show their own emotional commitment to the position they are advocating. Such expression is a delicate matter. If you act too emotional, people may doubt your clear headedness. But you must also show that your commitment to a goal is not just in your mind but in your heart and gut as well. Without this demonstration of feeling, people may wonder if you actually believe in the position you're championing.

Perhaps more important, however, is that effective persuaders have a strong and accurate sense of their audience's emotional state, and they adjust the tone of their arguments accordingly. Some- times that means coming on strong, with forceful points. Other times, a whisper may be all that is required. The idea is that whatever your position, you match your emotional fervour to your audience's ability to receive the message

Effective persuaders seem to have a second sense about how their colleagues have interpreted past events in the organization and how they will probably interpret a proposal. The best persuaders in our study would usually canvass key individuals who had a good pulse on the mood and emotional expectations of those about to be persuaded. They would ask those individuals how various proposals might affect colleagues on an emotional level – in essence, testing possible reactions. They were also quite effective at gathering information through informal conversations in the hallways or at lunch. In the end, their aim was to ensure that the emotional appeal behind their persuasion matched what their audience was already feeling or expecting.

To illustrate the importance of emotional match-making in persuasion, consider this example. The president of an aeronautics manufacturing company strongly believed that the maintenance costs and turnaround time of the company's U.S. and foreign competitors were so much better than his own company's that it stood to lose customers and profits. He wanted to communicate his fear and his urgent desire for change to his senior managers. So one afternoon, he called them into the boardroom. On an overhead screen was the projected image of a smiling man flying an old-fashioned biplane with his scarf blowing in the wind. The right half of the transparency was covered. When everyone was seated, the president explained that he felt as this pilot did, given the company's recent good fortune. The organization, after all, had just finished its most successful year in history. But then with a deep sigh, he announced that his happiness was quickly vanishing. As the president lifted the remaining portion of the sheet, he revealed an image of the pilot flying directly into a wall. The president then faced his audience and in a heavy voice said, "This is what I see happening to us." He asserted that the company was headed for a crash if people didn't take action fast. He then went on to lecture the group about the steps needed to counter this threat. The reaction from the group was immediate and negative. Directly after the meeting, managers gathered in small clusters in the hallways to talk about the president's "scare tactics." They resented what they perceived to be the president's overstatement of the case. As the managers saw it, they had exerted enormous effort that year to break the company's records in sales and profitability. They were proud of their achievements. In fact, they had entered the meeting expecting it would be the moment of recognition. But to their absolute surprise, they were scolded.

The president's mistake? First, he should have canvassed a few members of his senior team to ascertain the emotional state of the group. From that, he would have learned that they were in need of thanks and recognition. He should then have held a separate session devoted simply to praising the team's accomplishments. Later, in a second meeting, he could have expressed his own anxieties about the coming year. And rather than blame the team for ignoring the future, he could have calmly described what he saw as emerging threats to the company and then asked his management team to help him develop new initiatives.

Now let us look at someone who found the right emotional match with his audience: Robert Mar- cell, head of Chrysler's small-car design team. In the early 1990s, Chrysler was eager to produce a new subcompact – indeed, the company had not introduced a new model of this type since 1978. But senior managers at Chrysler did not want to go it alone. They thought an alliance with a foreign manufacturer would improve the car's design and protect Chrysler's cash stores.

Marcell was convinced otherwise. He believed that the company should bring the design and production of a new subcompact in-house. He knew that persuading senior managers would be difficult, but he also had his own team to contend with. Team members had lost their confidence that they would ever again have the opportunity to create a good car. They were also angry that the United States had once again given up its position to foreign competitors when it came to small cars.

Marcell decided that his persuasion tactics had to be built around emotional themes that would touch his audience. From innumerable conversations around the company, he learned that many people felt as he did – that to surrender the subcompact's design to a foreign manufacturer was to surrender the company's soul and, ultimately, its ability to provide jobs. In addition, he felt deeply that his organization was a talented group hungry for a challenge and an opportunity to restore its self-esteem and pride. He would need to demonstrate his faith in the team's abilities.

Marcell prepared a 15-minute talk built around slides of his hometown, Iron River, a now defunct mining town in Upper Michigan, devastated, in large part, by foreign mining companies. On the screen flashed recent photographs he had taken of his boarded-up high school, the shuttered homes of his childhood friends, the crumbling ruins of the town's ironworks, closed churches, and an abandoned railroad yard. After a description of each of these places, he said the phrase, "We couldn't com- pete" – like the refrain of a hymn. Marcell's point was that the same outcome awaited Detroit if the production of small cars was not brought back to the United States. Surrender was the enemy, he said, and devastation would follow if the group did not take immediate action.

Marcell ended his slide show on a hopeful note. He spoke of his pride in his design group and then challenged the team to build a "made-in-America" subcompact that would prove that the United States could still compete. The speech, which echoed the exact sentiments of the audience, rekindled the group's fighting spirit. Shortly after the speech, group members began drafting their ideas for a new car.

Marcell then took his slide show to the company's senior management and ultimately to Chrysler chairman Lee Iacocca. As Marcell showed his slides, he could see that Iacocca was touched. Iacocca, after all, was a fighter and a strongly patriotic man himself. In fact, Marcell's approach was not too different from Iacocca's earlier appeal to the United States Congress to save Chrysler. At the end of the show, Marcell stopped and said, "If we dare to be different, we could be the reason the U.S. auto industry survives. We could be the reason our kids and grandkids don't end up working at fast-food chains." Iacocca stayed on for two hours as Marcell explained in greater detail what his team was plan- ning. Afterward, Iacocca changed his mind and gave Marcell's group approval to develop a car, the Neon. With both groups, Marcell skillfully matched his emotional tenor to that of the group he was address- ing. The ideas he conveyed resonated deeply with his largely Midwestern audience. And rather than leave them in a depressed state, he offered them hope, which was more persuasive than promising doom. Again, this played to the strong patriotic sentiments of his American-heartland audience

No effort to persuade can succeed without emotion, but showing too much emotion can be as un- productive as showing too little. The important point to remember is that you must match your emotions to your audience's.

The concept of persuasion, like that of power, often confuses and even mystifies businesspeople. It is so complex – and so dangerous when mishandled – that many would rather just avoid it altogether. But like power, persuasion can be a force for enormous good in an organization. It can pull people together, move ideas forward, galvanize change, and forge constructive solutions. To do all that, however, people must understand persuasion for what it is – not convincing and selling but learning and negotiating. Furthermore, it must be seen as an art form that requires commitment and practice, especially as today's business contingencies make persuasion more necessary than ever.

How can HR gain the influence within the business that they deserve by 1) Know your audience and be prepared to speak their language) In order to be heard in HR you need to know your audience and what makes them take notice and listen. 2) Get involved:- It's all very well theorising and telling others what needs to be done, but you should be prepared and enthusiastic about actually getting involved in a practical sense. 3) Take backup:- It's always easier to convey a message and gain approval if you already have agreement from others. A united front from HR will help to increase influence over those that you're in discussions with. The old adage 'two heads are better than one' is true when it comes to fielding questions, researching a topic and preparing collateral that backs your proposals. 4) Lead by example:- As mentioned above, getting involved and being seen to taking an active part in a strategy is very important. One of the lasting effects is that people tend to respond to someone that leads by example. 5) Be 'human' is an important factor when it comes to building influence with colleagues. Unlike the online environment, in the real world, empathy, consideration and forethought are all traits that are respected and appreciated by colleagues. 6) Find and attract HR talent based on the above Building a team that reflects the qualities detailed above is key to maintaining and increasing influence that HR has with the rest of the business.

Resilient Leadership - Resilient individuals are able to sustain successful performance and positive wellbeing in the face of adverse conditions and to recover from or adjust easily to misfortune or change.

The next import area is How HR can be more resilient. Resilience at work can be described as the capability to maintain high performance and positive well-being. Resilient individuals are able to sustain successful performance and positive wellbeing in the face of adverse conditions, and to recover from or adjust easily to misfortune or change.

Resilience is a combination of personal characteristics and skills. Resilience skills are practical and can be learned and developed through appropriate training. The characteristics which are associated with higher levels of resilience are inherent in our personalities, however resilience skills can be used to help us adapt our natural style and tendencies.

ASSET is a model of workplace well-being which identifies requirements for us to feel good at work, for example the requirement to feel that we have the information and resources necessary to do our job. Our perceptions of situations at work are influenced by our personalities (as well as our attitudes, experience, etc.) and therefore our resilience in different circumstances will be

Robertson Cooper's model of resilience has four key components, all of which are influenced by our personality and the skills that we develop over time. Understanding these is the starting point for building your resilience and it is important to bear in mind that you are likely to have developed ways of overcoming hindrances to your resilience over time.

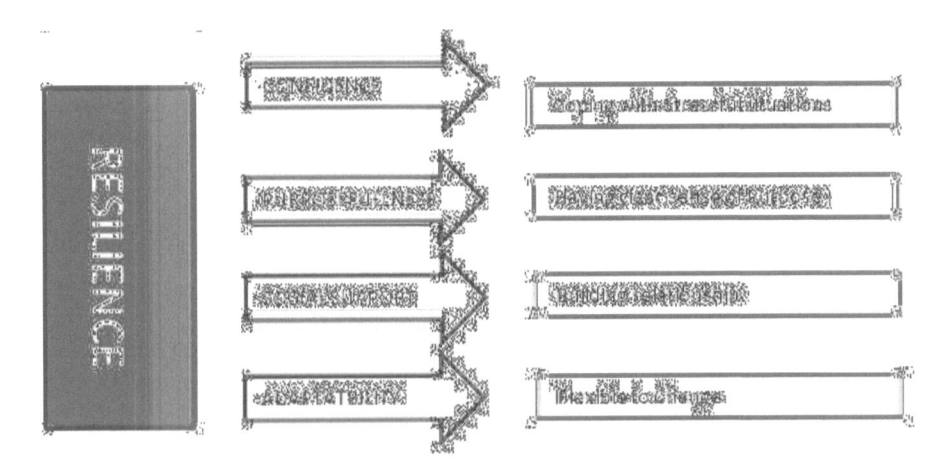

The four components of resilience are described below:-

Confidence: - Having feelings of competence, effectiveness in copying with stressful situations and strong self-esteem are inherent to feeling resilient. The frequency with which individuals experience positive and negative emotions is also key.

As a HR professional or as a Manager it is important for you to understand what Hinders your resilience and what Helps your resilience. There are few parameters where you should assess yourself like

LEVEL OF WORRY:- The extent to which you are likely to be anxious and worry about things depends very much on the situation in which you find yourself.

DEALING WITH DISTRESS:- You are prone to feeling sad or discouraged.

ANXIETY: Your confidence in interacting with others depends on the situation in which you find yourself; embarrassment or shyness when dealing with people is only occasionally a problem for you.

PRESSURE: You are not particularly confident in your ability to manage potentially stressful situations.

ENTHUSIASM: You are generally happy and optimistic, although your perspective may be more downbeat at times.

COMPLIANCE: You are generally confident in standing your ground on issues that you feel strongly about.

MODESTY: You view yourself positively in comparison to others and are proud of your achievements.

RESOURCEFULNESS: Your confidence in your own capability and resourcefulness is average and you may be inclined to underestimate the extent to which your skills and abilities will generalize to different situations.

PURPOSEFULNESS:- Having a clear sense of purpose, clear values, drive and direction help individuals to persist and achieve in the face of setbacks.

Similarly for Purposefulness you have to understand what Hinders your resilience and what helps. Parameters to be assessed are

ASSERTIVENESS: You are prepared to take the lead when necessary.

ACTIVITY: You are energetic and like to keep active and busy; you generally set a fast pace. **ADVENTUROUSNESS**: Your liking for excitement could be quite energizing for you, although it may also make you rather distractible and unfocused.

AESTHETICS: Artistic appreciation plays an important role in giving meaning to your life.

SOCIAL VALUES: Your strongly held personal values suggest that you have a clear sense of purpose.

SENSE OF DUTY: You are generally conscientious about adhering to ethical principles and fulfilling obligations.

AMBITION: You place little emphasis on achieving results for their own sake and are likely to be motivated only by specific goals that mean something to you.

SELF-DISCIPLINE: You sometimes find it difficult to sustain your efforts and to finish what you start.

DELIBERATION: You are cautious and deliberate, considering carefully what you want to achieve and how to go about it before acting.

SOCIAL SUPPORT:- Building good relationships with others and seeking support can help individuals overcome adverse situations, rather than trying to cope on their own. Parameters which has to be assessed for social support are

WARMTH: You tend to be formal and reserved in your relationships, and may keep your distance from some of the people who could provide useful social support in difficult times.

SOCIABILITY: You are likely to rely on a relatively small group of people for your social support; you may be inclined to draw mainly on your own resources rather than turning to others in difficult times.

TRUST: You are rather sceptical of other people's intentions, and careful about who you trust; this could limit your ability to draw on support when you need it.

STRAIGHTFORWARD: If you are too guarded about what you say, this could affect your ability to establish or draw on supportive relationships.

CONSIDERATION: You are generally considerate of others and responsive to requests for help, which makes it likely that this will be reciprocated by some of them when you need it.

ADAPTABILITY:- Flexibility and adapting to changing situations which are beyond our control are essential to maintaining resilience. Resilient individuals are able to cope well with change and their recovery from its impact tends to be quicker. what Hinders your resilience and what Helps your resilience are assessed by parameters as under

FRUSTRATION: Being prone to feelings of irritability and impatience may make it difficult for you to deal with problems and everyday frustrations in a calm and flexible manner.

IMPULSIVITY: Your self-control is average; you can control your response to respond to situations in a constructive, adaptable way but you may sometimes give in to your impulses.

IMAGINATION: You should be able to achieve a good balance between addressing immediate practicalities and looking ahead to anticipate future developments.

EMOTIONAL AWARENESS: Recognizing your own and others' emotional reactions should help you to respond adaptively in a changing situation.

VARIETY: Being open to variety and enjoying new and different activities will help you adapt to change and new situations.

IDEAS: Being generally open to new ideas should help your adaptability to different situations and demands.

SYMPATHY: Your sympathetic attitude should help the flexibility of your response as long as you do not put yourself under unnecessary pressure by being too sympathetic.

ORDER: You should be able to achieve a good balance between being organised and being flexible.

Resilience and the situational requirements for well-being at work.

When considering resilience, in addition to the role of our personality another important influence is the situation in which we find ourselves. The workplace presents many situations that test our resilience at times, and we will all respond to these in different ways. The next part is looking at the implications of your personality for your resilience in various situations at work. The ASSET model identifies six situational requirements necessary to achieve and maintain a state of positive well-being at work. These requirements are described below.

- **Informed and Equipped**:- Individuals feel that they have the information and resources they need to do their work.
- **Balanced Workload**:- Individuals feel their workload is stimulating but manageable.
- **Collaborative Relationships**:- Individuals feel encouraged and supported
- **In Control:- Individuals feel they have control and influence over how their work is done.**
- **Well-Managed Change**:- individuals experience change as positive and well-managed.
- **Sense of Purpose**:- Individuals have sense of purpose and feel that their goals are clear, challenging and achievable.

A HR head was once told to take a test of ASSET Model of wellbeing and this was his results. **The likely positives in different situations are as below...**

In situations where information or resources are limited: Thinking things through carefully may be helpful in deciding how to manage with what you have. Your active imagination will make it easier for you to come up with workaround solutions. You may welcome the opportunity to try out different approaches or ways of achieving your objectives.

When organizational change is creating a high level of challenge and uncertainty: Looking ahead and imagining different scenarios should help you to feel better prepared for what might happen. You are likely to be energised by the opportunity to try new activities or approaches, even if you are concerned about other aspects of the change and the way it is being managed.

In situations where goals are ill-defined and you need to create your own sense of purpose: Creating time and opportunities to follow your aesthetic interests is likely to help you to remain positive. Your need for variety should stimulate you to identify and pursue different activities. You are likely to spend time reviewing the information and guidance you have in order to clarify objectives and decide what you think is most important, and how to go about achieving this.

Possible Areas for HR Head to work on...

In situations where information or resources are limited: You are likely to be uncomfortable about taking action and making decisions if you feel you do not have enough time to consider, reflect and gather more information. You may become discouraged or de-motivated, and there is a risk that you will disengage or move on to something else without completing what needs to be done.

In situations where there are significant pressures on your workload or work life balance: There is a risk that you will become discouraged or give up too easily. You may need to make more effort than usual to engage with other people, so that you can share the load where possible.

When organisational change is creating a high level of challenge and uncertainty: Increasing the extent to which you actively seek out new ideas and information should help you to develop effective responses and creative solutions to new challenges. A sceptical view of human nature could lead you to become unduly concerned about other people's intentions in introducing or responding to the changes. You are likely to be uncomfortable with responding quickly to the situation as it develops, especially if information is limited.

In situations where work relationships are not as collaborative as might be expected: You may be too quick to become frustrated or irritable and this could escalate the situation, putting you under further pressure. Taking a more active interest in other people should help you to manage difficult relationships by understanding different perspectives and building rapport. Your reluctance to trust other people could lead you to take a rather pessimistic perspective of difficulties in work relationships. If you are too guarded about your objectives or concerns, this could make it difficult for you to ask for help or resolve issues with your work relationships.

In situations where goals are ill-defined and you need to create your own sense of purpose: You are likely to be motivated only by certain goals that you care about, so it will be important for you to identify these and ensure they are clearly defined and agreed. You are at risk of giving up or moving on to something else that catches your attention without putting in effort to define and pursue your goals.

In any difficult situation: There is a risk that you will put yourself under additional pressure by responding with greater impatience or annoyance than is warranted by the situation. Any strategies you can develop for managing pressure will be important for reducing your vulnerability to stress.

Once you take the test you may consider below questions to answer. Otherwise also once you read and understand Robertson Cooper theory you may like to answer these questions:

1. Which of the 6 situational factors do you find tests your resilience most?
2. Which of your 'likely positives' do you feel work particularly well for you?
3. Which could you make more use of to enhance your resilience?
4. Which of your 'possible areas to work' on have you already addressed to improve your resilience?
5. What are the 2-3 areas that you should priorities in order to further enhance your resilience?

Let us look at two case studies on Resilience leadership

Case Study 1

A well know Food Company which sells south Indian food products, Have seen a big opportunity in South Indian snacks, as one of the well know North Indian snacks giant was occupying almost 60% of South Indian snacks market and hence the management of South Indian Food company decided to launch south Indian snacks in South market as they were dominant in Food processed in Southern states of India. They did market survey, Consumer trials within small groups of consumers and launched the product in the market with adequate marketing strategies and visibility. Very soon the company realized that the product was not doing well in the market. This time they did a through consumer survey to find out that the crunchiness,taste was not adequate when compared with other competition products some went to the extend to say snacks were too oily.

The Company had to withdraw the products from market at the earliest, which was launched with a big visibility. The company realize that they did not have adequate technical competency in Research and development and operations for coming up with better snacky products as they were more of an food processing company and hence without much validating the products on different parameters launched in the market. They also realized that there was not much coordination between Marketing, R&D and Operations for deliberating on the products, trialing on the products before they launched.

Now the Organization realized its mistake and first and foremost got snacks expertize in research and development, Operations and Marketing and then formed a Collaborative Functional Team (CFT) consist of all core functions. The CFT team analyzed the core reasons of failure and then started working on the same in developing new products as per market requirements. Each and every function worked hard to bring best innovation in the products. Marketing team came up with new strategy to launch the product. And finally the product was re-launched with new taste, texture and strategy. The products were accepted in the market and started doing well. Today the Brand of snacks are doing well in market.

You can see how the management team showed resilience by understanding the mistakes committed and then taking fast and Innovative steps to make product success in the market.

Case Study 2

One of my know acquaintances named Shelly was working with this organization which is a cash management company, with a large number of Banks as their clientele. She was taking care of Business development. Shelly had a good experience of almost 16 years in Customer Services and Business Development in other organizations and hence she was selected to take care of the above profile. Looking at her performance and potential she was recommended by MD of the company to take over the role of "Customer Service Head" as there was a requirement of "Customer Services Head" for the existing customer services team of around 60 people that was being run in a stop-gap arrangement.

Hoping that it would be a cakewalk as Shelly has been handling various teams in different organizations for so many years, I took over this as a challenge. The Department had never a proper CS Head or a leader who would guide the team in terms of their deliverables and meeting the expectations of the clients. It was run in a matrix structure by a head from another function. Due to lack of exclusive attention as a department It was being in a total mismanaged uncontrollable condition. As a result, the quality of customer service was impacted which was unacceptable by clients. Well, this was the main reason for which it was decided by the management to now designate a Customer Service Head for the function.

Day 1:- A fresh start for Shelly in the new role. She was introduced to the team as their Head. It was quite an exciting day for her. I realized that day that no experience goes waste and no experience is enough to face a new challenge. Every day is a new beginning that gives new learning. The introduction with the team itself could make me feel that something is not right about the whole thing. I was not being welcomed; rather something not nice was waiting for me.

Day 2:- Second day of her new role. Trying to identify the key people with who to start my discussions and understandings of the team. The team had people working on a few levels. Base and foundation was the layer of " Customer Service Agents" whose main role was to attend to the customer queries and resolving them. The queries would come through calls and then they would be entered into the system as cases. There would be a specific time(Turn Around Time- TAT) to solve and get back to the client. The next level was the "Team Leader" who would take care of the team, their shifts, their performance monitoring, and ensure that the cases that they were solving were meeting TAT to be specific about the important KRAs as daily activities. Many more which were weekly and monthly. Moving towards the next level was the " Assistant Manager" who was responsible for monitoring the daily activities of the CS agents and the Team Leaders. Further going up the hierarchy was supposed to be the Customer Service Manager leading the whole team. This role was being handled by a Sunil(name changed), who had not much experience in Customer Service but was an old name in the whole team and had spent quite a good number of years in the system, that was his only strength. Shelly's interactions started with him. After spending an hour with him, she could sense that either he lacks knowledge of what was happening in the department or he is not ready to share information with her, this was the main reason that she spend the whole day with him to understand through various questions and different situations. Shelly was not clear whether Sunil was trying not to disclose what he knows or he doesn't know anything. Shelly tried all her leadership skills and experience but all went in vain as she couldn't get what she wanted from Sunil. A frustrating day for her, then to on the second day of her new role.

Day 3:- Third day was time to get things hands-on based on the discussion that Shelly had the day before with the acting CS Head. She has spent time with every member of the team in each shift along with the shift managers. To expect the least was timely action of the cases that were being registered in the system. Shelly was shocked to see that there was a huge backlog of cases with every CS agent. To her surprise, people were not even aware that the backlog was making the system slow, and then it was also affecting the TAT at the customer end. This had resulted in a huge amount of escalations which was again pending at the supervisor level. Shelly was sure that some escalation would have surely gone to the Head. Since there was no official contact of the Head, available at the customer end, most of it would get resolved over the telephone as and when the call would come to the Business Head. The whole team was working on a fire fighting situation. No wonder the MD was so desperate to have an experienced designated person to take charge. Shelly was happy then that she accepted the challenge. As an immediate course of action, she had a quick meeting with the Team Leaders and the managers in presence of the CS Head and chalked out a plan to ensure closure of all the old cases that had created the backlog. As that required immediate attention leaving everything else aside. To achieve that each one was required to give at least half an hour extra over and above their shift timings at least for a week. It was very important to have team spirit and understanding and commitment.

Day 4: A very special day ever for Shelly in her whole career. We will get to know very soon, why Shelly called it as a special day. Shelly was trying to gather all her observations and then make a report and sit with a detailed discussion to present my POA once my Boss was back from vacation. Shelly was confident that she will re-shape the whole thing completely. A huge task waiting to be executed. All Shelly had in hand was a team with no knowledge about their deliverable. Supervisors and managers who had no control over the team and the acting Head, with whom Shelly was still not clear whether he is not aware or doesn't want to share information. Here comes the shock. Shelly heard a familiar voice from Behind wishing "Good morning" to her it was Acting CS Head standing in front of her with the serious face as if wanting to tell Shelly something to scare her more than what he was sounding. Sunil with a rude voice said "They are saying they will not work" Nothing got into Shelly's head as she was busy with morning emails and other stuff. She asked. who?, he repeats himself being a little more specific, the team. The team refuses to work with a lady boss. Shelly didn't know what to say. Hearing something as baseless as this, she could have done only two things. Either react immediately or reach out to her boss. However, none of the options were suitable considering her years of experience she had to act than react. She requested some time from him to get back as she was amid some important mail to be answered. Shelly sat and thought of several options to act in this situation. Without losing any cool and remembering all the senior people who had ever been her mentor in my years of growth, zeroed down to only and only approach that could have fit to act in this situation. Shelly called Sunil for a discussion, It was pretty clear to her now that the problem was not with the team but Sunil himself. Sunil was trying to shoot keeping the gun on the team's shoulder. Shelly took a "Do or Die" approach to deal with the team. She gave him the first few minutes to talk and explain to in detail why the team has such a strong refusal to work with her. Sunil was again trying to explain Shelly that they are not ready to work with the lady boss. It was just not digestible to Shelly. It was not something to be even considered for discussion. She had to reach to the actual reason she started probing. then comes the second major reason for which the team was not happy, i.e, because Shelly has asked to stretch the working hours for half an hour extra for a few days till the backlog is removed. That was not all, Shelly was being told that they are not ready for any discussion. If they are forced to work beyond their shift, they would resign. Whatever has to be communicated has to be done through Sunil. Somehow Shelly was sure that these are not coming from the team. There must be some hidden agenda of Sunil. The team was too junior or maybe beginners to even think anything like this.

Without wasting much time Shelly gave two options to Sunil...... First option: Team member who has decided to resign for being asked to give extra time for the customer and company's sake can put their resignation on her table and walk out. If that has to start from Sunil himself, he can be the first one if he wishes to do so... Second option: Shelly said she is open for discussion if they want to continue to work. She also said that "he will not force anyone to work against their wish, but at the same time she can't continue to have a team who will not show up in the time of crisis". Shelly knew she was taking a risk. But at the same time, she knew that no HR or management can question her for asking any team member to work half an hour extra to complete the backlog. Her message was very loud and clear, and she showed a nonnegotiable attitude. She had a gut feeling that it would work. However Shelly was sure that Sunil will choose the second option. At times you should just let your intuitions work for you. Shelly was right.

Day 5 – Shelly started her meeting with the team. Considering shifts, she could not have the meeting with the whole team at the same time, hence met each one of them in a group of 5. None of the people she could see any expression or even a body language of revolt or non-acceptance. Rather they were very relieved that they have proper Team Head now. Yes, they have only one complaint that they were not being owned by anyone which had led to a lot of uncertainty and a sense of insecurity in them. Shelly could just see that in their eyes. It was so important for Shelly to build bonding with the team which could help her to walk with them. Successfully she completed meeting each one of them. she did not see any restlessness in those who were getting late to get back home as some of them had to wait beyond their shift timing. Shelly could very easily create a bond with them. She kept the discussion an open discussion and they were allowed to speak their heart out. That was enough for Shelly to win their confidence to kick start.

Day 6:- After the meeting with the base layer was over, Shelly met the Team Leaders and the Assistant Managers one by one. They had entirely a different story to share. More or less that matched with the customer service agents. One major reason was the lack of a proper leader and they were pretty upset with Sunil for making his own rules and running the show in his whims and fancies. He was a dictator and being very old in the system no one would dare to talk against him to anyone up in the hierarchy even if anyone had any disagreement. It was not possible to complete every discussion in one day. But Shelly could gather enough information to develop her plan of action.

It's said that a small misunderstanding can change everything. Shelly didn't mind being hated, but she always used to hate being misunderstood. It was a new beginning. The same set of people who had expressed their disagreement was showing acceptance.

This is a wonderful case of resilience. Shelly never gave up, even though she had pressure from her Boss to make the Customer service team productive in a short time and the unnecessary pressure exerted by Sunil misleading her about the team.

This chapter is quite a long chapter, but worth understanding. CHRO's/HR Heads should preach and practice these... Instrumental in developing Positive conflicts, encouraging fighting teams, developing a communication culture of openness and transparency, influencing The Art of persuasion and resilient leadership. These will help them to eradicate Sandwich situations and develop clear mindset role in the organization...

3

HR Doesn't Understand Business Expectations

Often, a wide gap exists between the HR strategy of an organization and what exactly is needed by the business strategy on the HR front. Since the talent of the right disposition and commitment is required to execute the strategy, misalignment does not let this happen. Those who can affect the alignment, they often come way ahead of others. Alignment here means that employees in the organization reflect all elements to help realize the strategy, e.g. skill, attitude, competencies, reward, recognition, satisfaction due to effective promotion policy, desired behavior to keep the customer satisfied, performance, requisite passion, team spirit, etc. Why do you think does non-alignment is often observed in actuality?

The need to align HR with the business has become more urgent than ever. Financial markets exert relentless pressure for growth, especially in emerging markets. Customers demand more and better service at a lower cost. And cost-efficiency, resource conservation, and regulatory compliance have become issues for almost every organization. Turnover among top talent is expected to increase in 2025; globalization is requiring stronger regional HR capabilities, and demographic shifts across the world are dramatically affecting the availability of qualified people.

Yet, all too often, business leaders still wonder aloud why their organizations even have HR departments. For their part, many HR leaders are willing to partner with the business, but given the unique situation of each company, they have little in the way of concrete guidance about how to fulfill that role.

Let me suggest a way to start. Of every action, you take as an HR leader, ask this simple question: does it cause friction in the business or does it create flow? Friction is anything that makes it more difficult for people in critical roles to win with the customer. Flow, on the other hand, is doing everything possible to remove barriers and promote better performance. The question applies to virtually any company in any business and it will take you farther down the road faster than the hazy, abstract injunction to become a strategic partner. Even in what appears to be routine HR responsibilities, you can inject the business perspective simply by asking whether what you are doing is going to enhance the flow of the business or impede it with friction.

Why is it so difficult to inject that business perspective? Because as HR leaders we feel ourselves to be near the pinnacle of the organization. The organization reports to *us*. It must meet our demands for information, documents, numbers. That's backward. We are far removed from the points and people that make a difference with customers and a difference to the business. Our perspective should be that of seeing to it that the people at those points can perform as smoothly, productively, and frictionless as possible.

Think, for example, of your talent strategy. Do you simply manage talent, or do you provide talent *solutions* that reduce friction and enhance the flow of the business? Often we pride ourselves on trying to recruit the best talent we can find and consistently and fairly spending our resources and focusing our attention equally on everyone. But does that enhance the flow of the business?

To truly be partners to the business we must identify those critical points of the business where the strategy succeeds or fails, and provide relevant talent solutions. In other words, we must think in terms of what Brian E. Becker, Mark A. Huselid, and Richard W. Beatty call "the differentiated workforce," in their book of the same name. That means managing talent as a portfolio of investments, some of which will pay a much higher return than others. Instead of spending an equal amount of time, attention, and resources on everyone equally, you make disproportionate investments in the most critical roles and critical people — not just in terms of compensation, but in terms of development, opportunities, retention, engagement, and human capital planning. All jobs in a business unit are important, but not all are strategic and have maximum impact on the economic value of the business.

Many business units spend time each year identifying talent and competency needs, but few get real about it by developing plans around winning in their critical talent spaces. Let's say you have, in your opinion, spent the appropriate amount of time identifying your strategic talent needs — the difference-making roles. Then ask yourself how much time you and your HR team and line leaders spend focusing on solutions for acquiring, developing, engaging, and retaining the talent to fill those needs? Or do you have the "equality" mentality — devoting the same amount of attention to everyone? It's shocking how many HR leaders say that their business has a strategic priority such as accelerating growth in emerging markets, but they and their teams spend little time in emerging markets. Does your investment of time and resources match your business strategy? If not, you are creating friction in the business that diminishes the strategic impact.

Inside CEO's Mind? What is CEO thinking on people's business function

A typical CEO of most of the organizations wants HR head to understand what is Business expecting out of people's function? How does he align Business goals with HR goals? How can HR be a true Talent Value leader? How can organizations have the best talent and pipeline of talents for better productivity? How can the Organization motivate employees to get the best out of them and retain the best talents? How can we use people analytics to drive business performance and how can we make our people process simple and easy to use?

This are the few expectations of the CEO of an organization. Let me discuss with you three important must-have qualities of a CHRO which the CEO expects. **Talent Value Leader (TVL), Chief Human Resources Analytical officer and Drive effective HR Operational excellence and continuous improvement.**

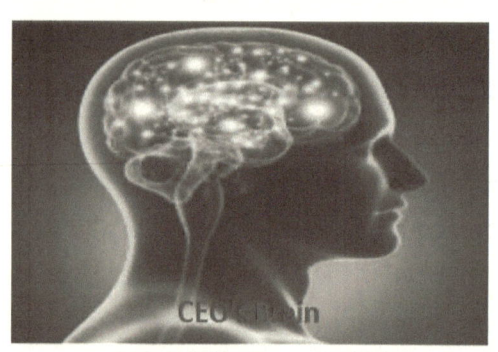

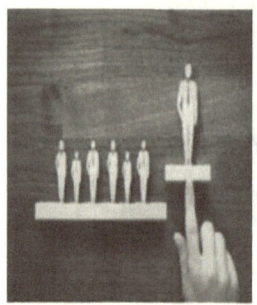

Talent Value Leader 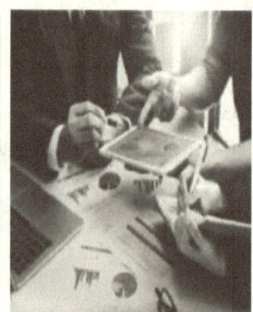   Analytics leader    HR Center of Excellence

Talent Value Leader (TVL)

The most important would be How can HR/HR Head be a Talent Value leader (TVL). A True TVL is one who can shape the talents of the organization to be a productive/performance leader. He is the custodian of the success profile of talents and leadership revolution for the organization. He advises functions on human resources strategy, analytics, foresees and plans the organization's future people strategy to make the organization future-ready. He has real authority over hiring and firing, even if actual decision rights remain with managers in the way actual spending decisions are taken by budget owners rather than being dictated by the finance function. Think of the manager of an IPL cricket Team who is responsible for allocating resources using acquisition, compensation, evaluation, development, motivation, and other levers to maximize the players' collective performance.

Unlike the typical HR business partner of today, TVs should be held to account using metrics that capture year-to-year skills development, capability gaps, engagement, and attrition. And to the maximum extent possible, they should be disconnected from the day-to-day concerns of operational HR so as not to get pulled back into dealing with employee issues—that means eliminating the HR liaison role that so many HR business partners play today.

TVLs, however, won't succeed without being able to deliver analytically driven talent insights to business managers systematically. This is a substantial change from today; while many HR business partners are resourceful and smart advisers to managers, few possess a data and analytical mind-set or the appropriate problem-solving tool kit.

When adopted, the expanded HR role we are describing starts to be taken seriously, as some companies are beginning to discover. A leading global materials company, for example, has been moving in this direction, specifying competencies for its HR leaders that now include the ability to "use analytics to diagnose and prescribe talent actions," to "translate talent decisions into profit-and-loss impact," and to "measure talent outcomes and their impact on value while holding managers accountable." The results have been significant. After an adjustment period, internal surveys show managers are substantially more satisfied with the support they receive from HR. Anecdotally, we also hear that more business leaders are scripting a role for their talent advisers during the strategic business-planning processes.

Chief Human Resources Analytical officer

How HR Head/CHRO can be a Chief Analytics Officer for human resources in the organization. How should he drive business performance through people analytics? Many organizations have already built extensive analytics capabilities, typically housed in centers of excellence with some combination of data-science, statistical, systems-knowledge, and coding expertise. Such CEOs often provide fresh insights into talent performance, but companies still complain that analytics teams are simple reporting groups—and even more often than they fail to turn their results into lasting value. What's missing, as a majority of North American CEOs indicated in a recent poll,[1] is the ability to embed data analytics into day-to-day HR processes consistently and to use their predictive power to drive better decision making.

In today's typical HR organization, most talent functions either implicitly or explicitly follow a process map; some steps are completed by business partners or generalists, others by HR shared services, and still others by COE specialists. Many of these steps require a recommendation or decision by a human being—for example, the evaluation of an employee's performance or the designation of a successor to a specific role.

Embedded analytics, by contrast, either inform or replace these steps with algorithms that leverage the data to drive fact-based insights, which are then directly linked to the deployment steps in the process. For example, many companies now use HR analytics to address attrition, allowing managers to predict which employees are most likely to leave and highlighting turnover problems in a region or country before the problem surfaces. By making the development and delivery of insights systematic, HR will start to drive strategic talent value in a more consistent way, rather than episodically and piecemeal as at present.

To understand more concretely the role of people analytics in an HR organization's journey toward a more strategic role, let's look closely at a single process—succession planning—and then assess the potential business impact of a broader suite of initiatives.

Analytics in action: Succession planning:- A standard approach starts with a talent-management or organizational-development COE laying out the process for the organization, designing the tools or templates, and training key stakeholders in what to do. Managers might then sit down with their HR partners and discuss potential succession candidates for key roles—ideally taking skills, competencies, and development pathways into account (in practice, of course, there may be a bit of "gut feel"). A traditional best-practice process would then create individual development plans for potential successors, based on the gap between that person and the potential role. As vacancies occur, these potential successors may or may not be tapped, much depending on whether the manager (or his or her HR partner) bothers to refer back to those plans.

An analytics-driven succession-planning process looks and feels very different. First, machine-learning algorithms might review years of succession data to understand success factors in a given role. Using that insight, the company might then derive the top five internal candidates for that role, accompanied by customized development plans (that is, what courses to take, what skills to build) based on their competencies. Such information would support subsequent strategic decisions, consultations between managers and strategic HR partners, and cross-functional assessments of enterprise bench strength.

The real prize is for those that can use data analytics not just to improve a single process, like recruitment or retention, but also to drive business performance—as has happened at a leading global quick-service restaurant business. The company mined data on employee personality traits, leadership styles, and working patterns and introduced changes that have improved customer service and had a tangible impact on financial performance

To achieve such an impact across the board, leaders will have to make significant investments in analytics skills and capabilities—but the returns should be commensurate. Based on a study of a range of industries with diverse workforces, operating models, and financial features, the McKinsey Global Institute estimates that companies using a portfolio of HR-analytics solutions could realize an increase of 275 basis points in profit margins, on average, by 2025. These increases will likely come about through productivity gains among front- and middle-office workers (which can translate into revenues or other increased-output opportunities) and through savings in recruiting, interviewing time, training, onboarding, and attrition costs.

Drive effective HR Operational excellence & continuous improvement.

The current reality of HR, as many business partners will attest, is that of the function routinely being pulled into operational issues and distracted from its core strategic mission. McKinsey research, indeed, shows that typical HR departments still spend close to 60 percent of their time and resources on transactional and operational HR, despite decades of pushing work out to shared services; the best-performing HR departments spend less than 40 percent of their time and resources on these transactional activities.

As part of its continuing transformation, HR must, therefore, raise service levels and improve the employee experience, using next-generation automation tools and standardized processes to drive higher productivity. There are three critical operational priorities for the HR organization of the future: continuous process improvement, next-generation automation technology, and user-experience-focused service improvement.

Continuous process improvement - Based on our work with companies, we see several ways to make HR operations more efficient—including finding further things that individuals and managers can do more easily themselves—notably by providing direct access to information or transactions online, introducing simpler processes, and ensuring clearer decision making. It's also worth considering more geographically diverse sourcing of work and talent, as a leading agricultural company did when it found deep pockets of high-end instructional design talent in several Indian cities. These people, it turned out, not only were less costly but proved themselves capable of delivering equal or better service than the relatively well-compensated instructional designers who had served the businesses previously, mostly from the United States and Western Europe. There is always scope for smarter sourcing of external vendors, whether through insourcing or outsourcing: one US insurance company, for example, improved its reliability and cut the overall cost of its payroll process in half by bringing it back in-house.

New automation technologies will soon reshape several HR processes, building on core human-resource-management-system platforms (both on-premises and in the cloud). Robotic process automation (RPA), smart workflows, cognitive agents, and natural-language processing, for example, will automate HR tasks previously carried out by people. The case of a leading global automotive-component manufacturer that was struggling with its employee-onboarding process is instructive. Thanks to the cross-functional complexity of the workflow, with different HR people needed to complete steps such as employee paperwork and scheduling orientation—and with IT, facilities, and security people needed to complete others—onboarding used to take weeks. RPA solved the problem with a bot that can access multiple systems, follow an intelligent workflow, and initiate communications. Onboarding time, on average, has been reduced by more than two-thirds, many errors created by manual tasks have been eliminated, and the journey has become more compelling for the individual.

What Business Wants? Expectations of CXOs from Business...

Core Functions and support functions have different expectations from the Human resources function from Talent Acquisition to Talent separation. Three most important expectations are

- How do HR act as an Advisor and Guide to them on people matters?
- How can HR be a an effective Human Resources Business Leader?
- How can HR help organization/function to make employees future ready?

Advisor and Guide: Functional head/Functional team most of the time look upon Human resources as a professional advisor and guide for all HR challenges. For that the first and foremost thing is building relationship. There is something called **"Active Constructive Responding"** ACR let me explain you what does ACR means.

Suppose one your friend asks you Hey! George I'm very glad to attend my sister's wedding next week, it is held in a fabulous destination will have a lots of fun. Immediately you respond to that saying "Ho! Yes last month I had my cousin sister's wedding that was the best weddings I have attend ever, lots of fun unlimited drinks food etc. You see how you have responded, don't one-up people in conversation if you want to develop a positive relationship with them. Let me give you one more example Your friend tells you nest week is my birthday I'm going to Goa in a resort on the water, going to have lots of fun, sea-foods, drinks etc You respond to him yes But this time in Goa it is going to be bad, bad weather, rough sea, even sea foods is bad now. What are you doing here you are discouraging him even though for you it may be for good. Avoid responding to someone's excitement with negativity or detractions. **Don't yuck their yum!** Another example is when someone is talking about something important or interesting you talk on a different topic, by these you are ignoring someone's talk. Don't respond to someone by changing the subject entirely and ignoring what they have shared with you. Another good example is suppose your friend says Next week I'm going to my ancestral house to see my grandma, it will be lots of fun, finally iam going for a vacation. You respond to them as Wow! That's great how are you going to spend time there, what are you plans, must be planning for a good foods, drinks, doing some adventure etc, tell me please I'm very excited to know. So here you are trying to be inquisitive, you are being engaged with him. Active Constructive Response is seeking to further the conversation, get more information, and encourage the other person with your response.

Similarly you have to build up relationship with the Functional heads/Dept heads for them to rely on you as an advisor/mentor. You must build relationships strong enough to bear the weight of truth and honesty. There are few quick wins you can do for them by solving issues which are critical for them. Functional heads look for people ideas/

strategies which can help them to solve their function people challenges. It is also a bonding between you and functions where you can rely on each other even when things are not rocky. Let me give you few cases where you can see how HR advice or guidance has helped the team.

Case 1

This is a case of one of the logistics company, where Ravi worked as Head Organization Development. He had joined few months back in the organization and was still getting accustom to systems and process of the Organization. While he bonded well with senior management team, the Chief Sales Officer was a difficult cookie, he somehow hated HR and was always trying to find faults with HR. Ravi make an impressive Annual Learning Calendar, which was liked by senior management team, but as usual he had problem as he thought this may not be right plan for sales team even though Ravi had detailed discussion with Senior Sales Managers and finally with him. The Chief Sales officer had a habit of agreeing personally and disagreeing publically. He was also not comfortable discussing his department issues with his Peer group or HR and always felt he can only handle any issues related to his function. The Organization was then going through a problem of high sales attrition. The company was losing field sales force on regular basis with an attrition of 45% per annum, even though the company was paying decent salary and incentives to the field sales force. The logistics company was going through growth phase and losing sales force at this time means losing sales. CEO was worried and asked Chief Sales Officer to take help of HR. Ravi spent time with CSO to understand the actual issue and what HR can do. Ravi after discussion with CSO confirmed that he was not fully aware what is making sales officers to leave the organization. He suggested CSO to allow him to conduct a survey on Sales officer, which for which he kind of agreed as he didn't have much choice though. After spending few weeks with Pan India Sales team, Ravi could analyze three prominent problems 1. Lack of robust incentive plan for retention of key performers. 2. Lack of career growth in the organization and new learning 3. No recognition for good work. While this is a common problem among sales organizations, but the main issue was lack of robust long term incentive plan for motivation to stay with the organization. The HR team worked out good career plans and rewards and recognition plans but what worked was the long term incentive plan. Ravi after doing good research work, talking to many companies and after discussing with internal opinion leaders come up with a Sales Retention Plan (SRP). This plan was simple but long term rewarding. What Ravi did is he worked out a long term incentive plan for 3 years where every year you achieve all 4 quarter targets your money doubles up in next year. You get paid in every quarter once you achieve your target. For First year you get incentive based on what you have achieved from second year this is how it was paid. see example below...

In case a person has completed his 2 years his, retention bonus can be

In case he achieves all his four quarter targets – (25,000+20,000)*4

In case he achieves his three quarter targets only – (25,000+15000)*3

In case he achieves his two quarter targets only – (25,000+5,000)*2

In case he achieves less than two quarter targets – 25,000

In case a person has completed his 3years, his retention bonus can be

In case he achieves all his four quarter targets – (40,000+20,000)*4

In case he achieves his three quarter targets only – (40,000+15,000)*3

In case he achieves his two quarter targets only – (40,000+5,000)*2

In case he achieves less than two quarter targets – 25,000

This plan was a hit in few months only because firstly you get paid every quarter and secondly the sales officer could see the big money he can earn end of 3 days if he is able to perform well. This has brought a completion with in sales officers and eventually the CSO could see the sales going up and attrition was also controlled. This made Ravi develop good confidence and Trust in the mind of CSO and he going ahead relied on Ravi for many guidance and advise.

As a Human Resources Business Partner:- The Functions expect HR to understand the challenges they face in business and help them to curve a strategy/solutions which can deliver faster and better results for their objectives. While there are many process for HRBP but the important factor is how can HR understand the needs of the function, that is possible only **"When you are able to walk in their shoes"** for which you need to be not only intellectually adept, but also emotionally attuned and aware. Also for you to understand them first you have to take off your shoes to be able to walk in their shoes. There may be lots of things going on in other person's world like workplace pressure, fear, vulnerabilities, assumptions, expectations, personal/family issues etc. You can walk in their (Functional Managers) shoes by sometimes getting personal – Sometimes the best way to get someone else to open up is to show vulnerability yourself. Get Curious, dig deeper to understand "Why" Tune into body language and test your assumption to validate your understanding and demonstrate you get him. Also look at course correction, ask yourself what can I do differently to know more about the person. This will help to understand your colleagues better. The next method would be **"How do you customize solutions for functional teams i.e Tailor it"** You feel good when you get something as per your need, like when a dress is made by your tailor and it fits perfectly as you want,you feel Wow! This is exactly the feeling functions feels when they get a tailor made solution. True fit can be achieved only when you adapt to the style of a particular person, the needs of the project, and the culture of the organization. How do you customize needs for the functions first you should know your style to focus on big picture, don't assume what your prefer is right for everyone. Secondly, Assess the situation - consider aspects like what is appropriate for the situation at hand? What are other persons preference and style? what are the dynamics of relationship? Thirdly, Check and refresh- Check by asking "Are you getting what you need from me? Remember if you feel sometimes it seems working now, might not work tomorrow. Fourth one is Adapt your style – Adapt as much as you need to while still being genuine. Be explicit about what you're doing so others know what to expect and can ask for more of what they need. It is also relevant to **"Change your thought process** "so called as Change the lens – Sometimes when your are stuck, what you need then is the new way of looking at things. When we change the lens, we challenge assumptions, reframe issues, and reveal new angles, bringing into focus realities and possibilities that weren't clear before. HR should consider 6 lenses for changing thought process 1. Look through someone else's eyes Competitor, customer, leadership, shareholder, colleague etc we are used to seeing the way things are from our own perspective, should try how others look at things. 2. The big picture:- It can be easy to get attached to a particular vantage point. People see their part but often lose sight of the whole. Zoom out and consider a larger field of vision. 3. The flip side There are multiple sides to every situation. Think opposite: Ask, "What would happen if we were to flip the current state of things around?" 4. The view from the future One way to break out of the paralysis of the here-and-now is to fast- forward to a future state. 5. The analogous angle Often, inspiration comes from applying the lessons of one context to another (e.g., What could an HMO learn from a retailer?). 6. The unexpected answer When you're trying to choose between options A, B, and C, it can be easy to forget that options X, Y, and Z even exist. Think about options or approaches that surprise and delight. The next moves would be to **Bring a point of view** – It so happens that many a times your functional colleagues just want to know what you think –straight up. They may need a specific recommendation. In those situations, it may not be about giving options, but about giving opinions. Informed guidance, delivered with conviction, can sometimes be exactly what's needed. Few tips which can help to bring a point of view are a) Be prepared to speak...You never know when you will have opportunity to present your point of view. Anticipate such moments and think what you might say that would genuinely help create that momentum, reduce uncertainty or guide the decision of the other person. Ask yourself... Would saying something now do any harm? Would not saying something now do any harm? b) Do your homework...Make sure you have evidence to support your recommendation, and be sure you have though few options that can be pulled out if appropriate. Ask yourself Do I know enough to provide useful insight, even if I don't have every detail figured out? Have I thought about what they're likely to ask? c) Anticipate their needs...You should prepare yourself anticipating what your functional team may ask like Is the near term what matters most right now? Are they in a position to talk about the future? d) Convey confidence... you have to demonstrate your level of confidence, Don't equivocate – convey your recommendation with confidence and conviction. Ask yourself... What assumptions did I make in reaching this perspective? What options did I rule out, and why? What else might I have failed to consider?

So for you to be a good HR Business leader you have to be Able to walk in your internal customer/functions shoes. Customize solutions for functional teams i.e Tailor it". Change your thought process/Change your lens and 4. Finally Bring appoint of view. There are many more like Suspend your self interest, Ownership of your views and actions, Say what no one else will etc but the above four is the important when you want to build a strong relationship with functions. Let me define a case study on effective Human Resources Business Partner.

Clare is Business leader in a multinational organization she an Management graduate with focus on Marketing, Finance and economy. She thinks about comsumer, Competition, Shareholder value, EBITDA, Sales Margin, Costs, Time to market. She recognizes people around her who are result oriented, has Analytical thinking, Communication skills and Problem solving skills.

We have second character called Steve, who is a HR professional, qualified in HR. What he thinks about is His internal customers, People solutions, Time to hire, Turnover and Employee costs. What he recognizes is Customer service, Effort and dedication, Integrity, Team work and New ideas.

Clare is interested in making business. She has to increase sales, both in value and volume, keep improving her margins, in order to meet the strategy and please her stakeholders. Mr. HR wants to help, but has not started speaking that much with Mrs. Business, so he does not come with that many impactful insights. To get things done, Clare would rather do it herself than involve Steve. Too bad, Steve really wanted to help.

To succeed with Clare, Steve must start by understanding what it is on her mind. He needs to understand How does the business group make money and provide value? How does the business group differentiate themselves from their competitors? Who are the key stakeholders internally and externally? How does the business measure and report on performance? What are the key Business imperatives and targets for the next 2-3 years? Steve approach Clare and says he will take care of the HR part as he nows understands her needs.

Clare saw Mr. H.R. as a helping hand to deal with her workforce. All she did not want to do, she gave to HR: pay, contract administration…

all that she needed to do to make employees come to work, and keep the authorities happy went into Steve's hands. It went on for a while.

Mr. HR took the job seriously, did it well, delivered reports, gave some useful insights... he hired people, gained confidence... Mrs. Business keeps growing her business. As her workforce grows, she gets problem she did not have before. Who can she talk to? A ha!!! Mr. HR, is the man with a(n HR) plan?

Mr. HR actually has a broad team working with him now, some well functioning processes, and good credibility in Clare's teams. Clare is confident she'll get some help, but looks at more effective ways to deliver the same service.

Clare's business is changing and HR have organized to best accommodate these needs, designing workforce and change solutions. Clare can rely on shared services to effectively manage the operational services, while line HR are now partners for the business. Clare notices an impact from HR who, with help of data, help reduce attrition, absenteeism, improve engagement and train leaders. They know "employee don't leave companies, they leave their managers". And HR is doing something about it.

Clare knows that change is just the new normal, that doing things faster and more efficiently simply won't suffice. She needs to do things differently and needs more than ever help in addressing change. She looks at Steve for help, since HR has been such a reliable partner so far, to make her business anytime change ready. Steve sees the organisation is lagging behind and understand HR needs to update its software. To get Digital.

Clare and Steve had a bonding of trust and from then they worked happily ever after. What Great HR looks like»

The Leadership Experience - Has a proactive advisor & challenger, providing her with data driven insights and helping her up her game and that of her organization

The Employee experience - Has easy access to tools & knowledge to drive her career forward, and answers to most of her queries are less than a click away

The HR Professional experience - Has acquired new skills, a broad set or roles to develop through – including from/to the business, as well as new digital colleagues

The Candidate Experience - Students and experiences professionals have a positive impression of the company before, during and after meeting them

The Alumni Experience - Has regular touch points with the company through which they can offer skills, bring business opportunities or talent

The Third Parties' Experience - Have the company on their Key Account list, because they are trend setters in their field and also because they are cool to work with.

Support Functions to make Talents future-ready

The expectation by the Business is raising day by day. Functions expect HR to be support them to make talent future ready. How HR helps functions in continuous up-skilling the talent to accomplish functional/organizational goals.

Why do we need skill up-gradation?

With the adaption of new technology, automization, new methods and innovations it is imperative that we should skill up the talents to prepare them for future growth. Today it has become a norm that if we don't upgrade ourselves with new innovation/technology/methods we will be obsolete soon and not stay relevant. The cycle of learn-unlearn-relearn is a true phenomenon today, we have to continuously keep learning unlearning and relearning. With the business going through dynamic changes due to market volatility we don't have a choice but to upgrade. Do you like to use the old technology mobile phones or laptops or computers, you will change to better technology and you will also adapt to the change fast. No one teaches you how to use smarts phone, you learn and get used to it soon. You always try to learn new things/technology saying good bye to old one. This is learn-unlearn and relearn. It is seen that only learning with not help, you have to empty cup and fill the cup again. Let me give you an example of learn-Unlearn and re-learn.

LEARN
UNLEARN
RELEARN

FIXED   GROWTH

MINDSETS

Learn Unlearn Relearn changes your mindset from fixed to growth mindset. A multinational company which was well known for foods products was planning to introduce jelly based candies particularly for kids in India. They did good research on the product and finally came up with what texture, taste, color and flavors the jelly based candies will look like. Now the challenge was production, as it takes almost 32 hours to get the final products, and you don't know when things change and you have to redo this again from the beginning. This was the first time when company was trying to introduce new category in the market and was extra cautious that things go well and consumer accept the product in market. After getting trained on the process the operations team started manufacturing, but in between they had many issues like the shape wasn't coming up well, in some cases the jelly was not getting evenly distributed. New Machines were brought for the production of the candies, but they have initial problems and had to stop production for weeks to rectify the technical slags. The manpower was kept idea for weeks till things were rectified, budgets were exceeding. The heating system and cooling system had to be aligned to fit the room temperature also get the right shape. It was process of learning the new process, unlearn few process and technics and re-learn the new process innovated process again. This process continued till they got the right shape, color, taste and feel. It was brought in the market, but then again consumers had views to look at options of different combination, pricing, packaging etc. The products went thought reverse engineering and was again launched in the market. This time the products was accepted very well. An excellent learning for the organization.

For Skill up-gradation it is imperative to understand the skill need analysis. Let me throw light on few of the component which analyses the needs.

1. Business context analysis: - The purpose of this analysis is to examine the organization, Business units, functions, departments and determine its basic business strategy, objectives and goals. In dealing with changing business environment, the organization analysis may focus on the company's new business goals and challenges, and the implications for jobs. In conducting organizational analysis, the company may consider issues like

    - Increased competition for old and new business
    - More demands for customized products
    - Greater emphasis on efficiency and cost reduction
    - Increased needs on cooperation among companies
    - Business strategies of the rival companies

- Merger, acquisition, diversification and expansion
- Automization and modernization
- Research and innovations etc

Organization analysis must also take into account the products and market diversification plans, growth plans in terms of volumes and geographical spreads. Modernization and computerization plans, outsourcing and contracting issues, quality improvement, and cost cutting and profit maximization proposals.

2. Task Analysis explains what must be done to perform a job or complete a process successfully. Task analysis(also called as knowledge, skill and attitude [KSA] analysis) means detailed examination of a job role to find out what are the knowledge, skill, attitude, motives, values and self-concept needed in people for superior or effective performance. Task analysis will determine what skills you would require in future. Every function should take up task analysis, with comparison of what current job skills and competences are and what is required role wise and job wise. For Blue collared employees supervisor should play a key role to identify future requirement in terms of skills and design skill matrix and for supervisors, engineers, executives their immediate Manager should identify. The process of task analysis are Develop a list of task statement, then develop a list of task clusters, develop a list of KSA's and then assess the importance of tasks.

3. Position Analysis...This is to know which position needs skill up-gradation and in which areas. In a function there may be few positions which doesn't need any up- gradation on skills, but few would need changes to meet business requirements. One of the best method to do position analysis is RASCI Model

(Responsibility, Accountable, Support, Control and Inform) This model clear helps to identify the key result areas and also modify according to the job performed so that there is no over lapping of jobs.

Barriers of skill up-gradation

1. Not sure what need to be upgraded on adapted:-

   Many a times the department or function is not sure what skills they wanted to upgrade. Sometimes business expectation are so volatile and dynamic that you don't know which areas you need skill up-gradation. For that the Business expectations should be clear first and then the functional and individual expectations which will kind of define what we are looking for. It is very important to do thing stage wise to get a better clarity

2. Skill up-gradation is not for me:-

   Functions/People feel that skill up-gradation is not meant for me as I know the best of my work and that will fetch organization best results. But they don't know what they don't no about the future requirement. People feel they are degraded if they say they don't know or wants to learn what they don't know. This barrier has to be taken out of people's mind. This is about will

3. I don't have qualification or knowledge for skill up-gradation:- This is about skill, even though they have will but don't have adequate skill and knowledge about skill required in future or even if they understand don't know is expectations out of them. This are people who can be trained for their good attitude, but not sure how much they would adapt to new skills.

4. Skill up-gradation may not help my function

   A similar one like I don't need skill up-gradation. This is from the function point of view where they say will my function be benefited by skill up-gradation. We are happy with what we have, what we need is improvement on that. While the organization wants its employees to acquire better skills, they wouldn't want them to spare them from their day to day work for skill up-gradation.

5. Costly affair, why should company invest on skill up-gradation:-

Many companies fail to understand amount spent on training/skill up-gradation is investments for future. They land up thinking more from cost angel rather than seeing big picture. For small investments now they may lose big opportunity in future in terms of Business for not having adequate skills or competencies. Some management also think skill up-gradation is not company's responsibility, it is individual responsibility, you up-grade or else we will hire new talents. Now this is not at all right approach for the Organization. This is not a story of a growing organization.

Boost employee motivation and engagement

If the company wants to be in Business they have to up-grade skills and competencies of the employees. The confidence of doing much better what you are doing or doing things differently needs courage. Employees have to learn new skills to achieve personal and organizational mile stone. Employees either have to be motivated or self-motivated to learn new skills/competencies in such a manner that they see a lot engagement being done at work which can enhance their future career aspirations. Sometime we are not sure whether the employee can upgrade their skills or not, for that organization should encourage them for developing new skills if they have the right motivation. Employees should have regular reviews, should be recognize for new learning's, provide all technical and more support to learn, allow movement in roles for better on the job learning, prioritize professional skill development, continuous mentoring programmers. These will boost his motivation to learn faster.

Help Building a learning organization - Deliver effective learning solutions

CHRO's should along with Functional Managers should analyze how they can build a learning organization by delivering effective learning solutions. Continuous improvement programs are sprouting up all over as organizations strive to better themselves and gain an edge. The topic list is long and varied, and sometimes it seems as though a program a month is needed just to keep up. Unfortunately, failed programs far outnumber successes, and improvement rates remain distressingly low. Why? Because most companies have failed to grasp a basic truth. Continuous improvement requires a commitment to learning.

How, after all, can an organization improve without first learning something new? Solving a problem, introducing a product, and reengineering a process all require seeing the world in a new light and acting accordingly. In the absence of learning, companies—and individuals—simply repeat old practices. Change remains cosmetic, and improvements are either fortuitous or short-lived.

A few farsighted Corporate executives have recognized the link between learning and continuous improvement and have begun to refocus their companies around it. Scholars too have jumped on the bandwagon, beating the drum for "learning organizations" and "knowledge-creating companies." In rapidly changing businesses like semiconductors and consumer electronics, these ideas are fast taking hold. Yet despite the encouraging signs, the topic in large part remains murky, confused, and difficult to penetrate.

Scholars' discussions of learning organizations have often been reverential and utopian, filled with near mystical terminology. Paradise, they would have you believe, is just around the corner. Peter Senge, who popularized learning organizations in his book *The Fifth Discipline,* described them as places "where people continually expand their capacity to create the results they truly desire, where new and expansive patterns of thinking are nurtured, where collective aspiration is set free, and where people are continually learning how to learn together."[1] To achieve these ends, Senge suggested the use of five "component technologies": systems thinking, personal mastery, mental models, shared vision, and team learning. In a similar spirit, Ikujiro Nonaka characterized knowledge-creating companies as places where "inventing new knowledge is not a specialized activity...it is a way of behaving, indeed, a way of being, in which everyone is a knowledge worker."[2] Nonaka suggested that companies use metaphors and organizational redundancy to focus thinking, encourage dialogue, and make tacit, instinctively understood ideas explicit.

Sound idyllic? Absolutely. Desirable? Without question. But does it provide a framework for action? Hardly. The recommendations are far too abstract, and too many questions remain unanswered. How, for example, will managers know when their companies have become learning organizations? What concrete changes in behavior are required? What policies and programs must be in place? How do you get from here to there?

Most discussions of learning organizations finesse these issues. Their focus is high philosophy and grand themes, sweeping metaphors rather than the gritty details of practice. Three critical issues are left unresolved; yet each is essential for effective implementation. First is the question of *meaning.* We need a plausible, well-grounded definition of learning organizations; it must be actionable and easy to apply. Second is the question of *management.* We need clearer guidelines for practice, filled with operational advice rather than high aspirations. And third is the question of *measurement.* We need better tools for assessing an organization's rate and level of learning to ensure that gains have in fact been made.

Once these **"three Ms"** are addressed, managers will have a firmer foundation for launching learning organizations. Without this groundwork, progress is unlikely, and for the simplest of reasons. For learning to become a meaningful corporate goal, it must first be understood.

Surprisingly, a clear definition of learning has proved to be elusive over the years. Organizational theorists have studied learning for a long time; the accompanying quotations suggest that there is still considerable disagreement (see the insert "Definitions of Organizational Learning"). Most scholars view organizational learning as a process that unfolds over time and link it with knowledge acquisition and improved performance. But they differ on other important matters.

Some, for example, believe that behavioural change is required for learning; others insist that new ways of thinking are enough. Some cite information processing as the mechanism through which learning takes place; others propose shared insights, organizational routines, even memory. And some think that organizational learning is common, while others believe that flawed, self-serving interpretations are the norm.

How can we discern among this cacophony of voices yet build on earlier insights? As a first step, consider the following definition:

A learning organization is an organization skilled at creating, acquiring, and transferring knowledge, and at modifying its behavior to reflect new knowledge and insights.

This definition begins with a simple truth: new ideas are essential if learning is to take place. Sometimes they are created de novo, through flashes of insight or creativity; at other times they arrive from outside the organization or are communicated by knowledgeable insiders. Whatever their source, these ideas are the trigger for organizational improvement. But they cannot by themselves create a learning organization. *Without accompanying changes in the way that work gets done, only the potential for improvement exists.*

This is a surprisingly stringent test for it rules out a number of obvious candidates for learning organizations. Many universities fail to qualify, as do many consulting firms. Even General Motors, despite its recent efforts to improve performance, is found wanting. All of these organizations have been effective at creating or acquiring new knowledge but notably less successful in applying that knowledge to their own activities. Total quality management, for example, is now taught at many business schools, yet the number using it to guide their own decision making is very small. Organizational consultants advise clients on social dynamics and small-group behavior but are notorious for their own infighting and factionalism. And GM, with a few exceptions (like Saturn and NUMMI), has had little success in revamping its manufacturing practices, even though its managers are experts on lean manufacturing, JIT production, and the requirements for improved quality of work life.

Organizations that do pass the definitional test—Honda, Corning, and General Electric come quickly to mind—have, by contrast, become adept at translating new knowledge into new ways of behaving. These companies actively manage the learning process to ensure that it occurs by design rather than by chance. Distinctive policies and practices are responsible for their success; they form the building blocks of learning organizations.

Learning Developing Blocks:- Learning organizations are skilled at five main activities: systematic problem solving, experimentation with new approaches, learning from their own experience and past history, learning from the experiences and best practices of others, and transferring knowledge quickly and efficiently throughout the organization. Each is accompanied by a distinctive mind-set, tool kit, and pattern of behavior. Many companies practice these activities to some degree. But few are consistently successful because they rely largely on happenstance and isolated examples. By creating systems and processes that support these activities and integrate them into the fabric of daily operations, companies can manage their learning more effectively.

1. Structured problem solving: -This first activity rests heavily on the philosophy and methods of the quality movement. Its underlying ideas, now widely accepted, include:

- Relying on the scientific method, rather than guesswork, for diagnosing problems (what Deming calls the "Plan, Do, Check, Act" cycle, and others refer to as "hypothesis-generating, hypothesis-testing" techniques).
- Insisting on data, rather than assumptions, as background for decision making (what quality practitioners call "fact-based management").
- Using simple statistical tools (histograms, Pareto charts, correlations, cause-and-effect diagrams) to organize data and draw inferences.

Most training programs focus primarily on problem-solving techniques, using exercises and practical examples. These tools are relatively straightforward and easily communicated; the necessary mind-set, however, is more difficult to establish. Accuracy and precision are essential for learning. Employees must therefore become more disciplined in their thinking and more attentive to details. They must continually ask, "How do we know that's true?", recognizing that close enough is not good enough if real learning is to take place. They must push beyond obvious symptoms to assess underlying causes, often collecting evidence when conventional wisdom says it is unnecessary.

Otherwise, the organization will remain a prisoner of "gut facts" and sloppy reasoning, and learning will be stifled.

Xerox has mastered this approach on a company-wide scale. In 1983, senior managers launched the company's Leadership through Quality initiative; since then, all employees have been trained in small-group activities and problem-solving techniques. Today a six-step process is used for virtually all decisions (see the insert "Xerox's Problem-Solving Process"). Employees are provided with tools in four areas: generating ideas and collecting information (brainstorming, interviewing, surveying); reaching consensus (list reduction, rating forms, weighted voting); analysing and displaying data (cause-and-effect diagrams, force-field analysis); and planning actions (flow charts, Gantt charts). They then practice these tools during training sessions that last several days. Training is presented in "family groups," members of the same department or business-unit team, and the tools are applied to real problems facing the group. The result of this process has been a common vocabulary and a consistent, companywide approach to problem solving. Once employees have been trained, they are expected to use the techniques at all meetings, and no topic is off-limits. When a high-level group was formed to review Xerox's organizational structure and suggest alternatives, it employed the very same process and tools.

2. Trail and Error:- This activity involves the systematic searching for and testing of new knowledge. Using the scientific method is essential, and there are obvious parallels to systematic problem solving. But unlike problem solving, experimentation is usually motivated by opportunity and expanding horizons, not by current difficulties. It takes two main forms: ongoing programs and one-of-a-kind demonstration projects. *Ongoing programs* normally involve a continuing series of small experiments, designed to produce incremental gains in knowledge. They are the mainstay of most continuous improvement programs and are especially common on the shop floor. Corning, for example, experiments continually with diverse raw materials and new formulations to increase yields and provide better grades of glass. Allegheny Ludlum, a specialty steelmaker, regularly examines new rolling methods and improved technologies to raise productivity and reduce costs.

Successful on-going programs share several characteristics. First, they work hard to ensure a steady flow of new ideas, even if they must be imported from outside the organization. Chaparral Steel sends its first-line supervisors on sabbaticals around the globe, where they visit academic and industry leaders, develop an understanding of new work practices and technologies, then bring what they've learned back to the company and apply it to daily operations. In large part as a result of these initiatives, Chaparral is one of the five lowest cost steel plants in the world. GE's Impact Program originally sent manufacturing managers to Japan to study factory innovations, such as quality circles and kanban cards, and then apply them in their own organizations; today Europe is the destination, and productivity improvement practices the target. The program is one reason GE has recorded productivity gains averaging nearly 5% over the last four years.

Successful ongoing programs also require an incentive system that favors risk taking. Employees must feel that the benefits of experimentation exceed the costs; otherwise, they will not participate. This creates a difficult challenge for managers, who are trapped between two perilous extremes. They must maintain accountability and control over experiments without stifling creativity by unduly penalizing employees for failures. Allegheny Ludlum has perfected this juggling act: it keeps expensive, high-impact experiments off the scorecard used to evaluate managers but requires prior approvals from four senior vice presidents. The result has been a history of productivity improvements annually averaging 7% to 8%.

Finally, ongoing programs need managers and employees who are trained in the skills required to perform and evaluate experiments. These skills are seldom intuitive and must usually be learned. They cover a broad sweep: statistical methods, like design of experiments, that efficiently compare a large number of alternatives; graphical techniques, like process analysis, that are essential for redesigning work flows; and creativity techniques, like storyboarding and role playing, that keep novel ideas flowing. The most effective training programs are tightly focused and feature a small set of techniques tailored to employees' needs. Training in design of experiments, for example, is useful for manufacturing engineers, while creativity techniques are well suited to development groups.

Demonstration projects are usually larger and more complex than ongoing experiments. They involve holistic, systemwide changes, introduced at a single site, and are often undertaken with the goal of developing new organizational capabilities. Because these projects represent a sharp break from the past, they are usually designed from scratch, using a "clean slate" approach. General Foods's Topeka plant, one of the first high-commitment work systems in this country, was a pioneering demonstration project initiated to introduce the idea of self-managing teams and high levels of worker autonomy; a more recent example, designed to rethink small-car development, manufacturing, and sales, is GM's Saturn Division.

Demonstration projects share a number of distinctive characteristics:
- They are usually the first projects to embody principles and approaches that the organization hopes to adopt later on a larger scale. For this reason, they are more transitional efforts

than endpoints and involve considerable "learning by doing." Mid-course corrections are common.
- They implicitly establish policy guidelines and decision rules for later projects. Managers must therefore be sensitive to the precedents they are setting and must send strong signals if they expect to establish new norms.
- They often encounter severe tests of commitment from employees who wish to see whether the rules have, in fact, changed.
- They are normally developed by strong multi-functional teams reporting directly to senior management. (For projects targeting employee involvement or quality of work life, teams should be multilevel as well.)
- They tend to have only limited impact on the rest of the organization if they are not accompanied by explicit strategies for transferring learning.

All of these characteristics appeared in a demonstration project launched by Copeland Corporation, a highly successful compressor manufacturer, in the mid-1970s. Matt Diggs, then the new CEO, wanted to transform the company's approach to manufacturing. Previously, Copeland had machined and assembled all products in a single facility. Costs were high, and quality was marginal. The problem, Diggs felt, was too much complexity.

At the outset, Diggs assigned a small, multifunctional team the task of designing a "focused factory" dedicated to a narrow, newly developed product line. The team reported directly to Diggs and took three years to complete its work. Initially, the project budget was $10 million to $12 million; that figure was repeatedly revised as the team found, through experience and with Diggs's prodding, that it could achieve dramatic improvements. The final investment, a total of $30 million, yielded unanticipated breakthroughs in reliability testing, automatic tool adjustment, and programmable control. All were achieved through learning by doing.

The team set additional precedents during the plant's start-up and early operations. To dramatize the importance of quality, for example, the quality manager was appointed second-in-command, a significant move upward. The same reporting relationship was used at all subsequent plants. In addition, Diggs urged the plant manager to ramp up slowly to full production and resist all efforts to proliferate products. These instructions were unusual at Copeland, where the marketing department normally ruled. Both directives were quickly tested; management held firm, and the implications were felt throughout the organization. Manufacturing's stature improved, and the company as a whole recognized its competitive contribution. One observer commented, "Marketing had always run the company, so they couldn't believe it. The change was visible at the highest levels, and it went down hard."

Once the first focused factory was running smoothly—it seized 25% of the market in two years and held its edge in reliability for over a decade—Copeland built four more factories in quick succession. Diggs assigned members of the initial project to each factory's design team to ensure that early learnings were not lost; these people later rotated into operating assignments. Today focused factories remain the cornerstone of Copeland's manufacturing strategy and a continuing source of its cost and quality advantages.

Whether they are demonstration projects like Copeland's or ongoing programs like Allegheny Ludlum's, all forms of experimentation seek the same end: moving from superficial knowledge to deep understanding. At its simplest, the distinction is between knowing how things are done and knowing why they occur. Knowing how is partial knowledge; it is rooted in norms of behavior, standards of practice, and settings of equipment. Knowing why is more fundamental: it captures underlying cause-and-effect relationships and accommodates exceptions, adaptations, and unforeseen events. The ability to control temperatures and pressures to align grains of silicon and form silicon steel is an example of knowing how; understanding the chemical and physical process that produces the alignment is knowing why.

Further distinctions are possible, as the insert "Stages of Knowledge" suggests. Operating knowledge can be arrayed in a hierarchy, moving from limited understanding and the ability to make few distinctions to more complete understanding in which all contingencies are anticipated and controlled. In this context, experimentation and problem solving foster learning by pushing organizations up the hierarchy, from lower to higher stages of knowledge.

3. Past Experience - Companies must review their successes and failures, assess them systematically, and record the lessons in a form that employees find open and accessible. One expert has called this process the "Santayana Review," citing the famous philosopher George Santayana, who coined the phrase "Those who cannot remember the past are condemned to repeat it." Unfortunately, too many managers today are indifferent, even hostile, to the past, and by failing to reflect on it, they let valuable knowledge escape.

A study of more than 150 new products concluded that "the knowledge gained from failures [is] often instrumental in achieving subsequent successes... In the simplest terms, failure is the ultimate teacher."[4] IBM's 360 computer series, for example, one of the most popular and profitable ever built, was based on the technology of the failed Stretch computer that preceded it. In this case, as in many others, learning occurred by chance rather than by careful planning. A few companies, however, have established processes that require their managers to periodically think about the past and learn from their mistakes.

Boeing did so immediately after its difficulties with the 737 and 747 plane programs. Both planes were introduced with much fanfare and also with serious problems. To ensure that the problems were not repeated, senior managers commissioned a high-level employee group, called Project Homework, to compare the development processes of the 737 and 747 with those of the 707 and 727, two of the company's most profitable planes. The group was asked to develop a set of "lessons learned" that could be used on future projects. After working for three years, they produced hundreds of recommendations and an inch-thick booklet. Several members of the team were then transferred to the 757 and 767 start-ups, and guided by experience, they produced the most successful, error-free launches in Boeing's history.

Boeing used lessons from earlier model development to help produce the 757 and 767—the most successful, error-free launches in its history. Other companies have used a similar retrospective approach. Like Boeing, Xerox studied its product development process, examining three troubled products in an effort to understand why the company's new business initiatives failed so often. Arthur D. Little, the consulting company, focused on its past successes. Senior management invited ADL consultants from around the world to a two-day "jamboree," featuring booths and presentations documenting a wide range of the company's most successful practices, publications, and techniques. British Petroleum went even further and established the post-project appraisal unit to review major investment projects, write up case studies, and derive lessons for planners that were then incorporated into revisions of the company's planning guidelines. A five-person unit reported to the board of directors and reviewed six projects annually. The bulk of the time was spent in the field interviewing managers.[5] This type of review is now conducted regularly at the project level.

At the heart of this approach, one expert has observed, "is a mindset that...enables companies to recognize the value of productive failure as contrasted with unproductive success. A productive failure is one that leads to insight, understanding, and thus an addition to the commonly held wisdom of the organization. An unproductive success occurs when something goes well, but nobody knows how or why."[6] IBM's legendary founder, Thomas Watson, Sr., apparently understood the distinction well. Company lore has it that a young manager, after losing $10 million in a risky venture, was called into Watson's office. The young man, thoroughly intimidated, began by saying, "I guess you want my resignation." Watson replied, "You can't be serious. We just spent $10 million educating you."

Fortunately, the learning process need not be so expensive. Case studies and post-project reviews like those of Xerox and British Petroleum can be performed with little cost other than managers' time. Companies can also enlist the help of faculty and students at local colleges or universities; they bring fresh perspectives and view internships and case studies as opportunities to gain experience and increase their own learning. A few companies have established computerized data banks to speed up the learning process. At Paul Revere Life Insurance, management requires all problem-solving teams to complete short registration forms describing their proposed projects if they hope to qualify for the company's award program. The company then enters the forms into its computer system and can immediately retrieve a listing of other groups of people who have worked or are working on the topic, along with a contact person. Relevant experience is then just a telephone call away.

4. Learning from others - Of course, not all learning comes from reflection and self-analysis. Sometimes the most powerful insights come from looking outside one's immediate environment to gain a new perspective. Enlightened managers know that even companies in completely different businesses can be fertile sources of ideas and catalysts for creative thinking. At these organizations, enthusiastic borrowing is replacing the "not invented here" syndrome. Milliken calls the process SIS, for "Steal Ideas Shamelessly"; the broader term for it is benchmarking. Enthusiastic borrowing is replacing the "not invented here" syndrome. According to one expert, "benchmarking is an ongoing investigation and learning experience that ensures that best industry practices are uncovered, analyzed, adopted, and implemented."7 The greatest benefits come from studying *practices,* the way that work gets done, rather than results, and from involving line managers in the process. Almost anything can be benchmarked. Xerox, the concept's creator, has applied it to billing, warehousing, and automated manufacturing. Milliken has been even more creative: in an inspired moment, it benchmarked Xerox's approach to benchmarking.

Unfortunately, there is still considerable confusion about the requirements for successful benchmarking. Benchmarking is not "industrial tourism," a series of ad hoc visits to companies that have received favorable publicity or won quality awards. Rather, it is a disciplined process that begins with a thorough search to identify best-practice organizations, continues with careful study of one's own practices and performance, progresses through systematic site visits and interviews, and concludes with an analysis of results, development of recommendations, and implementation. While time-consuming, the process need not be terribly expensive. AT&T's Benchmarking Group estimates that a moderate-sized project takes four to six months and incurs out-of-pocket costs of $20,000 (when personnel costs are included, the figure is three to four times higher).

Benchmarking is one way of gaining an outside perspective; another, equally fertile source of ideas is customers. Conversations with customers invariably stimulate learning; they are, after all, experts in what they do. Customers can provide up-to-date product information, competitive comparisons, insights into changing preferences, and immediate feedback about service and patterns of use. And companies need these insights at all levels, from the executive suite to the shop floor. At Motorola, members of the Operating and Policy Committee, including the CEO, meet personally and on a regular basis with customers. At Worthington Steel, all machine operators make periodic, unescorted trips to customers' factories to discuss their needs.

Customers can provide competitive comparisons and immediate feedback about service. And companies need these insights at all levels, from the executive suite to the shop floor. Sometimes customers can't articulate their needs or remember even the most recent problems they have had with a product or service. If that's the case, managers must observe them in action. Xerox employs a number of anthropologists at its Palo Alto Research Center to observe users of new document products in their offices. Digital Equipment has developed an interactive process called "contextual inquiry" that is used by software engineers to observe users of new technologies as they go about their work. Milliken has created "first-delivery teams" that accompany the first shipment of all products; team members follow the product through the customer's production process to see how it is used and then develop ideas for further improvement.

Learning organizations cultivate the art of open, attentive listening. Managers must be open to criticism. Whatever the source of outside ideas, learning will only occur in a receptive environment. Managers can't be defensive and must be open to criticism or bad news. This is a difficult challenge, but it is essential for success. Companies that approach customers assuming that "we must be right, they have to be wrong" or visit other organizations certain that "they can't teach us anything" seldom learn very much. Learning organizations, by contrast, cultivate the art of open, attentive listening.

5. Knowledge Transfer - For learning to be more than a local affair, knowledge must spread quickly and efficiently throughout the organization. Ideas carry maximum impact when they are shared broadly rather than held in a few hands. A variety of mechanisms spur this process, including written, oral, and visual reports, site visits and tours, personnel rotation programs, education and training programs, and standardization programs. Each has distinctive strengths and weaknesses. Reports and tours are by far the most popular mediums. Reports serve many purposes: they summarize findings, provide checklists of dos and don'ts, and describe important processes and events. They cover a multitude of topics, from benchmarking studies to accounting conventions to newly discovered marketing techniques. Today written reports are often supplemented by videotapes, which offer greater immediacy and fidelity.

Tours are an equally popular means of transferring knowledge, especially for large, multidivisional organizations with multiple sites. The most effective tours are tailored to different audiences and needs. To introduce its managers to the distinctive manufacturing practices of New United Motor Manufacturing Inc. (NUMMI), its joint venture with Toyota, General Motors developed a series of specialized tours. Some were geared to upper and middle managers, while others were aimed at lower ranks. Each tour described the policies, practices, and systems that were most relevant to that level of management.

Despite their popularity, reports and tours are relatively cumbersome ways of transferring knowledge. The gritty details that lie behind complex management concepts are difficult to communicate secondhand. Absorbing facts by reading them or seeing them demonstrated is one thing; experiencing them personally is quite another. As a leading cognitive scientist has observed, "It is very difficult to become knowledgeable in a passive way. Actively experiencing something is considerably more valuable than having it described."[8] For this reason, personnel rotation programs are one of the most powerful methods of transferring knowledge.

In many organizations, expertise is held locally: in a particularly skilled computer technician, perhaps, a savvy global brand manager, or a division head with a track record of successful joint ventures. Those in daily contact with these experts benefit enormously from their skills, but their field of influence is relatively narrow. Transferring them to different parts of the organization helps share the wealth. Transfers may be from division to division, department to department, or facility to facility; they may involve senior, middle, or first-level managers. A supervisor experienced in just-in-time production, for example, might move to another factory to apply the methods there, or a successful division manager might transfer to a lagging division to invigorate it with already proven ideas. The CEO of Time Life used the latter approach when he shifted the president of the company's music division, who had orchestrated several years of rapid growth and high profits through innovative marketing, to the presidency of the book division, where profits were flat because of continued reliance on traditional marketing concepts.

Line to staff transfers are another option. These are most effective when they allow experienced managers to distill what they have learned and diffuse it across the company in the form of new standards, policies, or training programs. Consider how PPG used just such a transfer to advance its human resource practices around the concept of high-commitment work systems. In 1986, PPG constructed a new float-glass plant in Chehalis, Washington; it employed a radically new technology as well as innovations in human resource management that were developed by the plant manager and his staff. All workers were organized into small, self-managing teams with responsibility for work assignments, scheduling, problem solving and improvement, and peer review. After several years running the factory, the plant manager was promoted to director of human resources for the entire glass group. Drawing on his experiences at Chehalis, he developed a training program geared toward first-level supervisors that taught the behaviors needed to manage employees in a participative, self-managing environment.

As the PPG example suggests, education and training programs are powerful tools for transferring knowledge. But for maximum effectiveness, they must be linked explicitly to implementation. All too often, trainers assume that new knowledge will be applied without taking concrete steps to ensure that trainees actually follow through. Seldom do trainers provide opportunities for practice, and few programs consciously promote the application of their teachings after employees have returned to their jobs.

Xerox and GTE are exceptions. As noted earlier, when Xerox introduced problem-solving techniques to its employees in the 1980s, everyone, from the top to the bottom of the organization, was taught in small departmental or divisional groups led by their immediate superior. After an introduction to concepts and techniques, each group applied what they learned to a real-life work problem. In a similar spirit, GTE's Quality: The Competitive Edge program was offered to teams of business-unit presidents and the managers reporting to them. At the beginning of the 3-day course, each team received a request from a company officer to prepare a complete quality plan for their unit, based on the course concepts, within 60 days. Discussion periods of two to three hours were set aside during the program so that teams could begin working on their plans. After the teams submitted their reports, the company officers studied them, and then the teams implemented them. This GTE program produced dramatic improvements in quality, including a recent semifinalist spot in the Baldrige Awards.

GTE proved knowledge is more likely to be transferred effectively when the right incentives are in place. The GTE example suggests another important guideline: knowledge is more likely to be transferred effectively when the right incentives are in place. If employees know that their plans will be evaluated and implemented—in other words, that their learning will be applied—progress is far more likely. At most companies, the status quo is well entrenched; only if managers and employees see new ideas as being in their own best interest will they accept them gracefully. AT&T has developed a creative approach that combines strong incentives with information sharing. Called the Chairman's Quality Award (CQA), it is an internal quality competition modeled on the Baldrige prize but with an important twist: awards are given not only for absolute performance (using the same 1,000-point scoring system as Baldrige) but also for improvements in scoring from the previous year. Gold, silver, and bronze Improvement Awards are given to units that have improved their scores 200, 150, and 100 points, respectively. These awards provide the incentive for change. An accompanying Pockets of Excellence program simplifies knowledge transfer. Every year, it identifies every unit within the company that has scored at least 60% of the possible points in each award category and then publicizes the names of these units using written reports and electronic mail.

How do you measure learning

CHRO's and Functional Managers have long known that "if you can't measure it, you can't manage it." This maxim is as true of learning as it is of any other corporate objective. Traditionally, the solution has been "learning curves" and "manufacturing progress functions." Both concepts date back to the discovery, during the 1920s and 1930s, that the costs of airframe manufacturing fell predictably with increases in cumulative volume. These increases were viewed as proxies for greater manufacturing knowledge, and most early studies examined their impact on the costs of direct labor. Later studies expanded the focus, looking at total manufacturing costs and the impact of experience in other industries, including shipbuilding, oil refining, and consumer electronics. Typically, learning rates were in the 80% to 85% range (meaning that with a doubling of cumulative production, costs fell to 80% to 85% of their previous level), although there was wide variation.

Firms like the Boston Consulting Group raised these ideas to a higher level in the 1970s. Drawing on the logic of learning curves, they argued that industries as a whole faced "experience curves," costs and prices that fell by predictable amounts as industries grew and their total production increased. With this observation, consultants suggested, came an iron law of competition. To enjoy the benefits of experience, companies would have to rapidly increase their production ahead of competitors to lower prices and gain market share.

Both learning and experience curves are still widely used, especially in the aerospace, defense, and electronics industries. Boeing, for instance, has established learning curves for every work station in its assembly plant; they assist in monitoring productivity, determining work flows and staffing levels, and setting prices and profit margins on new airplanes. Experience curves are common in semiconductors and consumer electronics, where they are used to forecast industry costs and prices.

For companies hoping to become learning organizations, however, these measures are incomplete. They focus on only a single measure of output (cost or price) and ignore learning that affects other competitive variables, like quality, delivery, or new product introductions. They suggest only one possible learning driver (total production volumes) and ignore both the possibility of learning in mature industries, where output is flat, and the possibility that learning might be driven by other sources, such as new technology or the challenge posed by competing products. Perhaps most important, they tell us little about the sources of learning or the levers of change.

Another measure has emerged in response to these concerns. Called the "half-life" curve, it was originally developed by Analog

Devices, a leading semiconductor manufacturer, as a way of comparing internal improvement rates. A half-life curve measures the time it takes to achieve a 50% improvement in a specified performance measure. When represented graphically, the performance measure (defect rates, on-time delivery, time to market) is plotted on the vertical axis, using a logarithmic scale, and the time scale (days, months, years) is plotted horizontally. Steeper slopes then represent faster learning (see the insert "The Half-Life Curve" for an illustration).

The Half-Life Curve Analog Devices has used half-life curves to compare the performance of its divisions. Here monthly data on customer service are graphed for seven divisions. Division C is the clear winner: even though it started with a high proportion of late deliveries, its rapid learning rate led eventually to the best absolute performance. Divisions D, E, and G have been far less successful, with little or no improvement in on-time service over the period. Source: Ray Stata, "Organizational Learning—The Key to Management Innovation," Sloan Management Review, Spring 1989, p. 72.

The logic is straightforward. Companies, divisions, or departments that take less time to improve must be learning faster than their peers. In the long run, their short learning cycles will translate into superior performance. The 50% target is a measure of convenience; it was derived empirically from studies of successful improvement processes at a wide range of companies. Half-life curves are also flexible. Unlike learning and experience curves, they work on any output measure, and they are not confined to costs or prices. In addition, they are easy to operationalize, they provide a simple measuring stick, and they allow for ready comparison among groups.

Yet even half-life curves have an important weakness: they focus solely on results. Some types of knowledge take years to digest, with few visible changes in performance for long periods. Creating a total quality culture, for instance, or developing new approaches to product development are difficult systemic changes. Because of their long gestation periods, half-life curves or any other measures focused solely on results are unlikely to capture any short-run learning that has occurred. A more comprehensive framework is needed to track progress.

Organizational learning can usually be traced through three overlapping stages. The first step is cognitive. Members of the organization are exposed to new ideas, expand their knowledge, and begin to think differently. The second step is behavioral. Employees begin to internalize new insights and alter their behavior. And the third step is performance improvement, with changes in behavior leading to measurable improvements in results: superior quality, better delivery, increased market share, or other tangible gains. Because cognitive and behavioral changes typically precede improvements in performance, a complete learning audit must include all three.

Surveys, questionnaires, and interviews are useful for this purpose. At the cognitive level, they would focus on attitudes and depth of understanding. Have employees truly understood the meaning of self-direction and teamwork, or are the terms still unclear? At PPG, a team of human resource experts periodically audits every manufacturing plant, including extensive interviews with shop-floor employees, to ensure that the concepts are well understood. Have new approaches to customer service been fully accepted? At its 1989 Worldwide Marketing Managers' Meeting, Ford presented participants with a series of hypothetical situations in which customer complaints were in conflict with short-term dealer or company profit goals and asked how they would respond. Surveys like these are the first step toward identifying changed attitudes and new ways of thinking.

To assess behavioural changes, surveys and questionnaires must be supplemented by direct observation. Here the proof is in the doing, and there is no substitute for seeing employees in action. Domino's Pizza uses "mystery shoppers" to assess managers' commitment to customer service at its individual stores; L.L. Bean places telephone orders with its own operators to assess service levels. Other companies invite outside consultants to visit, attend meetings, observe employees in action, and then report what they have learned. In many ways, this approach mirrors that of examiners for the Baldrige Award, who make several-day site visits to semifinalists to see whether the companies' deeds match the words on their applications.

Finally, a comprehensive learning audit also measures performance. Half-life curves or other performance measures are essential for ensuring that cognitive and behavioral changes have actually produced results. Without them, companies would lack a rationale for investing in learning and the assurance that learning was serving the organization's ends.

Learning organizations are not built overnight. Most successful examples are the products of carefully cultivated attitudes, commitments, and management processes that have accrued slowly and steadily over time. Still, some changes can be made immediately. Any company that wishes to become a learning organization can begin by taking a few simple steps.

The first step is to foster an environment that is conducive to learning. There must be time for reflection and analysis, to think about strategic plans, dissect customer needs, assess current work systems, and invent new products. Learning is difficult when employees are harried or rushed; it tends to be driven out by the pressures of the moment. Only if top management explicitly frees up employees' time for the purpose does learning occur with any frequency. That time will be doubly productive if employees possess the skills to use it wisely. Training in brainstorming, problem solving, evaluating experiments, and other core learning skills is therefore essential.

Another powerful lever is to open up boundaries and stimulate the exchange of ideas. Boundaries inhibit the flow of information; they keep individuals and groups isolated and reinforce preconceptions. Opening up boundaries, with conferences, meetings, and project teams, which either cross organizational levels or link the company and its customers and suppliers, ensures a fresh flow of ideas and the chance to consider competing perspectives. General Electric CEO Jack Welch considers this to be such a powerful stimulant of change that he has made "boundarylessness" a cornerstone of the company's strategy for the 1990s.

Once managers have established a more supportive, open environment, they can create learning forums. These are programs or events designed with explicit learning goals in mind, and they can take a variety of forms: strategic reviews, which examine the changing competitive environment and the company's product portfolio, technology, and market positioning; systems audits, which review the health of large, cross-functional processes and delivery systems; internal benchmarking reports, which identify and compare best-in-class activities within the organization; study missions, which are dispatched to leading organizations around the world to better understand their performance and distinctive skills; and jamborees or symposiums, which bring together customers, suppliers, outside experts, or internal groups to share ideas and learn from one another. Each of these activities fosters learning by requiring employees to wrestle with new knowledge and consider its implications. Each can also be tailored to business needs. A consumer goods company, for example, might sponsor a study mission to Europe to learn more about distribution methods within the newly unified Common Market, while a high-technology company might launch a systems audit to review its new product development process.

Together these efforts help to eliminate barriers that impede learning and begin to move learning higher on the organizational agenda. They also suggest a subtle shift in focus, away from continuous improvement and toward a commitment to learning. Coupled with a better understanding of the "three Ms," the meaning, management, and measurement of learning, this shift provides a solid foundation for building learning organizations.

Digitization across functions

Bringing analytics to life is about few norms which organization should follow for effective data driven organization

1: Start simple, with existing data

With the increased buzz around the Internet of Things (IoT) in manufacturing, many companies are excited about deploying thousands of low-cost sensors within their operations. While we do think this idea shows value, our experience shows that most of the data currently being generated is unused (exhibit). Simple analytics, done right, and with the existing treasure trove of data can yield tremendous value for manufacturers in the near term. Those early victories help win the hearts and minds of frontline employees while strengthening a data-driven decision culture—and the business case for further advanced-analytics investment.

2: Capture the right data, not just more data

Having the right data is more important than having lots of data. One basic-materials company invested several million dollars installing a "smart" manufacturing system that tracked more than a million variables. When the company analyzed 500 data tags from the system pertaining to a specific analytical use case, however, half of them were shown to hold limited or duplicated information. Another 25 percent of the data was discarded by a panel of process experts and data scientists as not being helpful for analytics. Further into the exploratory-analysis stage, the company found 20 critical variables—including a key dependent variable—that were not being measured, making precise predictive analytics impossible. This formed the case for deploying new sensors in a targeted fashion within the plant, while the company used analytics to provide critical decision-support tools for the process engineers as a first step in a quest to increase yield by 1 percent.

3: Don't let the long-term perfect be the enemy of the short-term good

Missing data can threaten to stall analytics projects while they wait for a multiyear data architecture transformation. We acknowledge that capturing the full value of IoT-driven advanced analytics will require an investment in the technology stack. But companies don't have to be bogged down by long IT projects. Minor investments can deliver much value.

One no-regret move is to develop a "data lake"—a flexible way to integrate data across an enterprise and overcome silo-based data management without full centralization. Although data lakes need strong governance and accountability for data definition and quality, they can democratize data access. Typically, data lakes provide data to different user groups either by permitting access to raw data or through data distillation, which affords access to pre-defined data structures.

The development approach required to implement analytics adds to the case for an alternative IT architecture. Analytical experimentation and exploration require agile software-development methods with daily or weekly release cycles. This short cadence is often a challenge for established IT processes and data infrastructure. The solution is a parallel "fast-speed" IT and data infrastructure, often a cloud-based system offering a range of deployment environments and tailored databases.

Data lakes and cloud solutions get companies' analytics efforts off to a faster start, allowing them to develop, test, and implement new use cases quickly. That helps in the creation of the necessary proof of concept before the wider rollout of new solutions. It is also a valuable way to build the organization's analytical muscles as people become accustomed to new ways of working and decision making using analytics.

4: Focus on outcomes, not technology

Investment in digital products and solutions without knowing how they will deliver meaningful impact will lead to frustrating discussions with business leaders. An approach based on use cases can help (Sidebar, "Successful analytics use cases"). When defining a use case, be sure to answer four fundamental questions together with their follow-ups:

What is the desired business outcome? Is it a new business opportunity, a cost-reduction opportunity, an increase in innovation capacity?

What are the value levers? Should the focus be on energy savings, more-efficient maintenance, higher asset utilization, lower inventory, higher throughput?

What technical requirements must the proposed approach meet for it to scale across the organization? Are new data sources needed? How will the solution integrate with legacy IT systems? How will we handle the volume of data securely? What analytical techniques will be used? What new dashboards are required?

How will the approach fit into our existing processes? Who will use the new system? What behaviors and decision-making processes must change to take turn analytical insights into business outcomes?

5: Look for value across activities as well as within them

While advanced-analytics methods have been applied very successfully to many specific activities that take place within the four walls of a manufacturing plant, much of the value of digitization lies in the whitespaces between organizational siloes—by bridging the gap between design and manufacturing, manufacturing and the supply network, and finally connecting with the end user. A manufacturer of highly specialized equipment recently conducted a "digital thread diagnostic" that identified more than $300 million of actionable productivity improvements that could be realized with using better data flow between design and manufacturing, real-time performance management, and other levers.

6: Break out of the pilot trap

A pilot project is a powerful, and important, way to demonstrate the value of advanced analytics, build momentum, and encourage buy-in. Capturing that value, however, means scaling the approach across the entire company. That's hard, and failure to scale can turn supporters into critics very quickly. Leaders must therefore think through the full end-to-end journey needed to turn attractive use cases into widespread impact. Some common pitfalls:

Focusing on the technology or approach, rather than the real source of value. When defining the use case, it is important to start with the true source of value, which is often the user or customer needs. A software tool is almost never a panacea; moreover, the selection of the right technology depends on the universe of use cases a company wants to deploy.

Solving for one use case at a time: Focusing too closely on a single use case can lead to choices that limit scalability later on. Important technical requirements to achieve scale include advanced operational and analytical data architecture, such as data lakes and data-search layers, together with IoT platforms, tools for digitization and analytics, and a repository of modeling tools and techniques.

In a factory setting, the right IoT platform can help analyze many functions regardless of the specific application, and thereby scale a variety of use cases at once. The underlying technology needs are essentially the same whether the organization is trying to optimize yield or to predict failure of critical equipment. An IoT platform can provide common capabilities for computing power or storage or security, while reducing the cost of developing and maintaining applications.

In assessing IoT platform needs, companies should bear five factors in mind: the application environment and the proposed platform's connectivity to existing IT infrastructure; the platform's ability to ingest high-velocity and-variety data streams while providing context to the data; its compatibility with a broader enterprise-cloud strategy; data sovereignty and security questions; and its capacity for edge processing and control, meaning it allows for processing and data storage close to the source, rather than only centrally.

Prematurely celebrating success: Companies should think through the entire end-to-end journey, beyond the technical elements needed to achieve scale beyond a single proof of concept. Data-governance issues such as domains, critical data elements, accountability models, and role definitions can pose tricky organizational and personnel questions, especially given the new analytical and technical positions that may be required. And analytics-generated insights must be integrated into existing workflows, often with attendant changes to business processes.

Nailing the technical solution, but forgetting the people: Technology is exciting—but it's people who capture the impact. While analytics can point to the right answer, people must act differently to capture the impact. Capturing the digital opportunity is a team sport, requiring close, cross-functional collaboration. A team of people with deep process knowledge, analytical acumen, and IT experience must work together to frame the problem, translate the business problem into an analytical problem, and define the right system and technical requirements from an IT perspective. Translating the analytical output into a form that can be used at the front line, and changing frontline behavior to make use of that new information, requires knowledge of human factors, persuasive design and change-management experience. Some companies find it useful to create a new role—digital translator—at the intersection of process knowledge, data science, and IT, to bring the required cross-functional teams together and steer the analytics effort from concept to bottom-line impact.

To avoid these pitfalls, companies need a structured approach to manage their analytics efforts, identifying and managing a pipeline of use cases, for example, and building the right technology stack. Once a use case is selected, companies need to systematically plan, pilot, scale, and embed analytics into their everyday processes through large-scale change management and capability building.

7: Build your capabilities

The application of analytics at scale will require organizational changes, too. For example, a company needs to define its talent strategy as new roles and new career paths emerge. There will be a need for data scientists, agile IT teams, and user experience (UX) designers, who play a crucial role in supporting real-world use of analytics. A persuasive design created with frontline involvement, is often the secret to high adoption levels for any analytical solution. Accordingly, UX professionals should be involved from the moment a use case is designed, not asked to apply a visual interface after a solution has largely been built.

In addition, a company needs "translators"—multi-skilled individuals who can shepherd the process from end to end. Translators need deep business knowledge and the ability to get into the workflow of operations and maintenance teams. They must be comfortable with analytics and able to challenge data scientists. They must understand IT systems and design thinking. And they must be able to communicate impact to the leadership team. That's a very tough combination of skills to find.

In addition to these internal roles, a clear partnership strategy is important. There is an explosion of both big companies and start-ups with unique IoT capabilities. The successful companies will very quickly home in on their unique value proposition and partner in areas that help accelerate their capabilities.

The potential impact from IoT-driven advanced analytics is game changing. While it is easy for companies to get started and get some quick wins on the board, it is much harder to scale across the company and deliver consistent bottom-line impact. The most successful organizations will be those that think through all of the implications, invest in both technology and people, forge smart partnerships, and maintain sufficient leadership appetite to persist.

People Analytics

More than 70% of companies now say they consider people analytics to be a high priority. The field even has celebrated case studies, like Google's Project Oxygen, which uncovered the practices of the tech giant's best managers and then used them in coaching sessions to improve the work of low performers. Other examples, such as Dell's experiments with increasing the success of its sales force, also point to the power of people analytics.

But hype, as it often does, has outpaced reality. The truth is, people analytics has made only modest progress over the past decade. A survey by Tata Consultancy Services found that just 5% of big-data investments go to HR, the group that typically manages people analytics. And a recent study by Deloitte showed that although people analytics has become mainstream, only 9% of companies believe they have a good understanding of which talent dimensions drive performance in their organizations.

What gives? If, as the sticker says, people analytics teams have charts and graphs to back them up, why haven't results followed? We believe it's because most rely on a narrow approach to data analysis: They use data only about individual people, when data about the interplay *among* people is equally or more important.

People's interactions are the focus of an emerging discipline we call *relational analytics*. By incorporating it into their people analytics strategies, companies can better identify employees who are capable of helping them achieve their goals, whether for increased innovation, influence, or efficiency. Firms will also gain insight into which key players they can't afford to lose and where silos exist in their organizations.

Most people analytics teams rely on a narrow approach to data analysis. Fortunately, the raw material for relational analytics already exists in companies. It's the data created by e-mail exchanges, chats, and file transfers—the *digital exhaust* of a company. By mining it, firms can build good relational analytics models.

Paul Leonardi and Noshir Contractor in their article in Harvard Business Review present a framework for understanding and applying relational analytics. And they have the charts and graphs to back us up.

Relational Analytics: A Deeper Definition

To date, people analytics has focused mostly on employee *attribute* data, of which there are two kinds:

Trait: facts about individuals that don't change, such as ethnicity, gender, and work history.

State: facts about individuals that do change, such as age, education level, company tenure, value of received bonuses, commute distance, and days absent.

The two types of data are often aggregated to identify group characteristics, such as ethnic makeup, gender diversity, and average compensation.

Attribute analytics is necessary but not sufficient. Aggregate attribute data may seem like relational data because it involves more than one person, but it's not. Relational data captures, for example, the communications between two people in different departments in a day. In short, relational analytics is the science of human social networks.

Decades of research convincingly show that the relationships employees have with one another—together with their individual attributes—can explain their workplace performance. The key is finding "structural signatures": patterns in the data that correlate to some form of good (or bad) performance. Just as neurologists can identify structural signatures in the brain's networks that predict bipolar disorder and schizophrenia, and chemists can look at the structural signatures of a liquid and predict its kinetic fragility, organizational leaders can look at structural signatures in their companies' social networks and predict how, say, creative or effective individual employees, teams, or the organization as a whole will be.

The Six Signatures of Relational Analytics

Drawing from our own research and our consulting work with companies, as well as from a large body of other scholars' research, we have identified six structural signatures that should form the bedrock of any relational analytics strategy.

Let's look at each one in turn.

Ideation

Most companies try to identify people who are good at ideation by examining attributes like educational background, experience, personality, and native intelligence. Those things are important, but they don't help us see people's access to information from others or the diversity of their sources of information—both of which are arguably even more important. Good idea generators often synthesize information from one team with information from another to develop a new product concept. Or they use a solution created in one division to solve a problem in another. In other words, they occupy a brokerage position in networks.

Ideation Signature

Focus: Individual

Predicts: Which employees will come up with good ideas

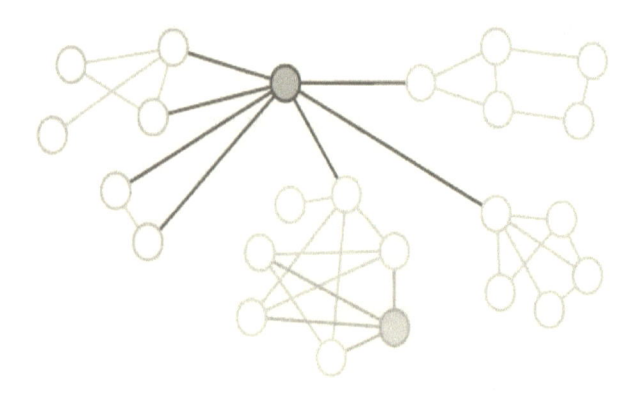

Purple shows *low constraint*: He communicates with people in several other networks besides his own, which makes him more likely to get novel information that will lead to good ideas. Orange, who communicates only with people within his network, is less likely to generate ideas, even though he may be creative.

The sociologist Ronald Burt has developed a measure that indicates whether someone is in a brokerage position. Known as *constraint,* it captures how limited a person is when gathering unique information. Study after study, across populations as diverse as bankers, lawyers, analysts, engineers, and software developers, has shown that employees with low constraint—who aren't bound by a small, tight network of people—are more likely to generate ideas that management views as novel and useful.

In one study, Burt followed the senior leaders at a large U.S. electronics company as they applied relational analytics to determine which of 600-plus supply chain managers were most likely to develop ideas that improved efficiency. They used a survey to solicit such ideas from the managers and at the same time gather information on their networks. Senior executives then scored each of the submitted ideas for their novelty and potential value.

The only attribute that remotely predicted whether an individual would generate a valuable idea was seniority at the company, and its correlation wasn't strong. Using the ideation signature—low constraint—was far more powerful: Supply chain managers who exhibited it in their networks were significantly more likely to generate good ideas than managers with high constraint.

A study Paul did at a large software development company bolsters this finding. The company's R&D department was a "caveman world." Though it employed more than 100 engineers, on average each one talked to only five other people. And those five people typically talked only to one another. Their contact with other "caves" was limited.

Such high-constraint networks are quite common in organizations, especially those that do specialized work. But that doesn't mean low-constraint individuals aren't hiding in plain sight. At the software company, relational analytics was able to pinpoint a few engineers who did span multiple networks. Management then generated a plan for encouraging them to do what they were naturally inclined to, and soon saw a significant increase in both the quantity—and quality—of ideas they proposed for product improvements.

Influence

Developing a good idea is no guarantee that people will use it. Similarly, just because an executive issues a decree for change, that doesn't mean employees will carry it out. Getting ideas implemented requires influence.

But influence doesn't work the way we might assume. Research shows that employees are not most influenced, positively or negatively, by the company's senior leadership. Rather, it's people in less formal roles who sway them the most.

Influence Signature

Focus: Individual

Predicts: Which employees will change others' behavior

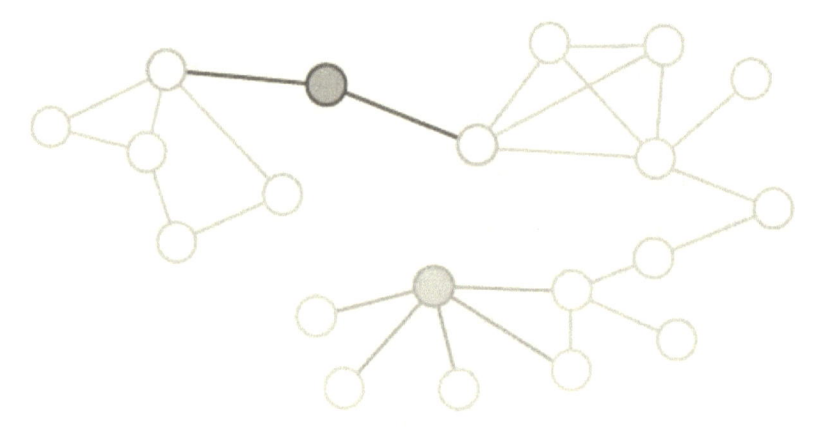

Though she connects to only two people, purple is more influential than orange, because purple's connections are better connected. Purple shows *higher aggregate prominence*. Orange may spread ideas faster, but purple can spread ideas further because her connections are more influential.

If that's the case, executives should just identify the popular employees and have them persuade their coworkers to get on board with new initiatives, right? Wrong.

A large medical device manufacturer that Paul worked with tried that approach when it was launching new compliance policies. Hoping to spread positive perceptions about them, the change management team shared the policies' virtues with the workers who had been rated influential by the highest number of colleagues. But six months later employees still weren't following the new procedures.

Why? A counterintuitive insight from relational analytics offers the explanation: Employees cited as influential by a large number of colleagues aren't always the most influential people. Rather, the greatest influencers are people who have strong connections to others, even if only to a few people. Moreover, their strong connections in turn have strong connections of their own with other people. This means influencers' ideas can spread further.

The structural signature of influence is called *aggregate prominence*, and it's computed by measuring how well a person's connections are connected, and how well the connections' connections are connected. (A similar logic is used by search engines to rank-order search results.)

Employees are not most influenced by the company's senior leadership.

In each of nine divisions at the medical device manufacturer, relational analytics identified the five individuals who had the highest aggregate prominence scores. The company asked for their thoughts on the new policies. About three-quarters viewed them favorably. The firm provided facts that would allay fears of the change to them as well as to the influencers who didn't like the policies—and then waited for the results.

Six months later more than 75% of the employees in those nine divisions had adopted the new compliance policies. In contrast, only 15% of employees had adopted them in the remaining seven affected divisions, where relational analytics had not been applied.

Efficiency

Staffing a team that will get work done efficiently seems as if it should be simple. Just tap the people who have the best relevant skills.

Efficiency Signature

Focus: Team

Predicts: Which teams will complete projects on time

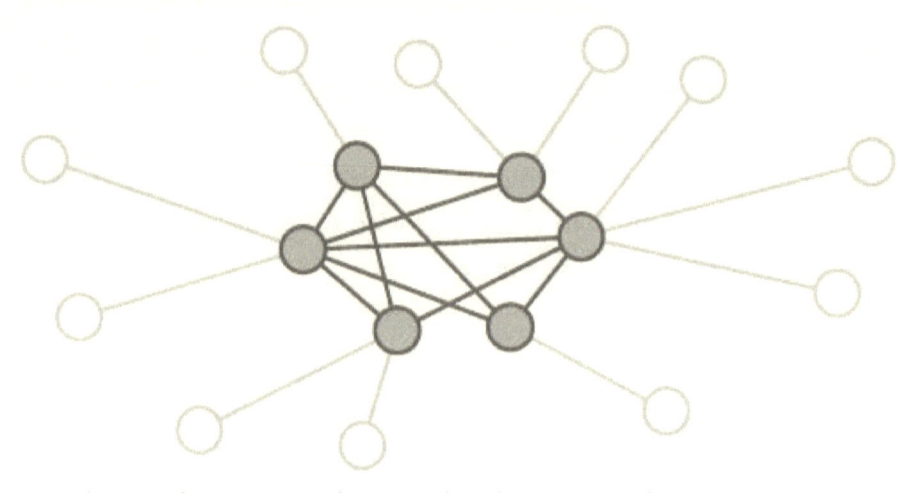

The purple team members are deeply connected with one another—showing *high internal density*. This indicates that they work well together. And because members' external connections don't overlap, the team has *high external range*, which gives it greater access to helpful outside resources.

Attribute analytics can help identify skilled people, but it won't ensure that the work gets done on time. For that, you need relational analytics measuring team chemistry and the ability to draw on outside information and expertise.

Consider the findings of a study by Ray Reagans, Ezra Zuckerman, and Bill McEvily, which analyzed more than 1,500 project teams at a major U.S. contract R&D firm. Hypothesizing that the ability to access a wide range of information, perspectives, and resources would improve team performance, the researchers compared the effect of demographic diversity on teams' results with the effect of team members' social networks. One issue was that diversity at the firm had only two real variables, tenure and function. (The other variables—race, gender, and education—were consolidated within functions.) Nevertheless, the results showed that diversity in those two areas had little impact on performance.

A slight increase in internal density and external range would save 2,200 hours.

Turning to the relational data, though, offered better insight. The researchers found that two social variables were associated with higher performance. The first was *internal density,* the amount of interaction and interconnectedness among team members. High internal density is critical for building trust, taking risks, and reaching agreement on important issues. The second was the *external range* of team members' contacts. On a team that has high external range, each member can reach outside the team to experts who are distinct from the contacts of other members. That makes the team better able to source vital information and secure resources it needs to meet deadlines. The structural signature for efficient teams is therefore high internal density plus high external range.

At the R&D firm the teams that had this signature completed projects much faster than teams that did not. The researchers estimated that if 30% of project teams at the firm had internal density and external range just one standard deviation above the mean, it would save more than 2,200 labor hours in 17 days—the equivalent of completing nearly 200 additional projects.

Innovation

Teams with the efficiency signature would most likely fail as innovation units, which benefit from some disagreement and strife.

Innovation Signature

Focus: Team

Predicts: Which teams will innovate effectively

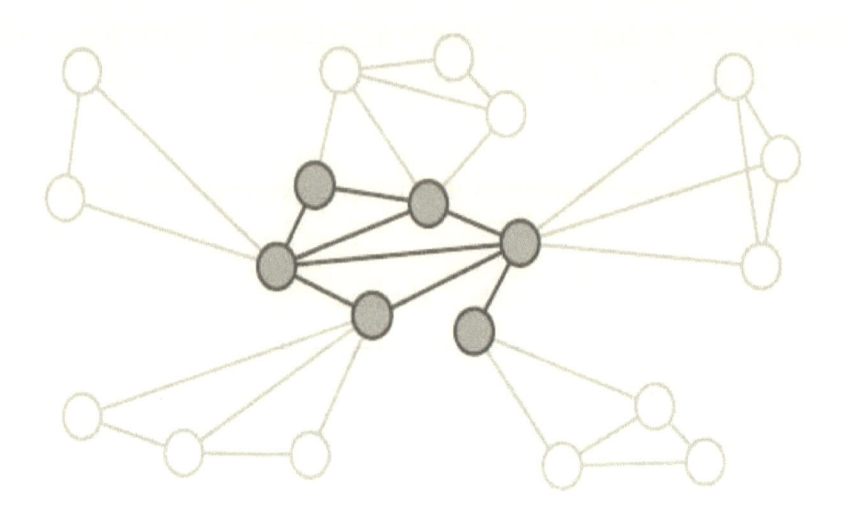

Purple team members aren't deeply interconnected; their team has *low internal density*. This suggests they'll have different perspectives and more-productive debates. The members also have *high external range*, or wide, diverse connections, which will help them gain buy-in for their innovations.

What else makes for a successful team of innovators? You might think that putting your highest-performing employees together would produce the best results, but research suggests that it might have negative effects on performance. And while the conventional wisdom is that teams are more creative when they comprise members with different points of view, research also indicates that demographic diversity is not a good predictor of team innovation success. In our experience, even staffing an innovation team with ideators often produces no better than average performance.

But if you turn to relational analytics, you can use the same variables you use for team efficiency—internal density and external range—to create promising innovation teams. The formula is a bit different, though: The innovation signature is high external range and low internal density. That is, you still want team members with wide, nonoverlapping social networks (influential ones, if possible) to source diverse ideas and information. But you do not want a tight-knit team.

Why? Greater interaction within a team results in similar ways of thinking and less discord. That's good for efficiency but not for innovation. The most innovative teams have disagreements and discussion—sometimes even conflict—that generate the creative friction necessary to produce breakthroughs.

The high external range is needed not just to bring in ideas but also to garner support and buy-in. Innovation teams have to finance, build, and sell their ideas, so well-connected external contacts who become the teams' champions can have a big impact on their success.

For several years, Paul worked with a large U.S.-based automobile company that was trying to improve its product-development process. Each of its global product-development centers had a team of subject-matter experts focused on that challenge. The program leader noted, "We are very careful about who we select. We get the people with the right functional backgrounds, who have consistently done innovative work, and we make sure there is a mix of them from different backgrounds and that they are different ages." In other words, the centers used attribute analytics to form teams.

Managers at a new India center couldn't build a demographically diverse team, however: All the center's engineers were roughly the same age, had similar backgrounds, and were about the same rank. So the manager instead chose engineers who had worked on projects with different offices and worked in different areas of the center—creating a team that naturally had a higher external range.

It so happened that such a team showed lower internal density as well. Its members felt free to debate, and they ran tests to resolve differences of opinion. Once they found a new procedure, they went back to their external connections, using them as influencers who could persuade others to validate their work.

After three years the India center's team was producing more process innovations than any of the other teams. After five years it had generated almost twice as many as all the other teams combined. In response, the company began supplementing its attribute analytics with relational analytics to reconfigure the innovation teams at its other locations.

Silos

Everyone hates silos, but they're natural and unavoidable. As organizations develop deep areas of expertise, almost inevitably functions, departments, and divisions become less and less able to work together. They don't speak the same technical language or have the same goals.

Silo Signature

Focus: Organization

Predicts: Whether an organization is siloed

Each color indicates a department. People within the departments are deeply connected, but only one or two people in any department connect with people in other departments. The groups' *modularity*—the ratio of internal to external communication—is high.

We assess the degree to which an organization is siloed by measuring its *modularity*. Most simply, modularity is the ratio of communication within a group to communication outside the group. When the ratio of internal to external communication is greater than 5:1, the group is detrimentally siloed.

One of the most strikingly siloed organizations we've encountered was a small not-for-profit consumer advocacy group, which wanted to understand why traffic on its website had declined. The 60 employees at its Chicago office were divided among four departments: business development, operations, marketing and PR, and finance. Typical of silos, each department had different ideas about what was going on.

Analysis showed that all four departments exceeded the 5:1 ratio of internal to external contacts. The most extreme case was operations, with a ratio of 13:1. Of course, operations was the department with its finger most squarely on the pulse of consumers who visited the site. It sat on a trove of data about when and why people came to the site to complain about or praise companies.

Other departments didn't even know that operations collected that data. And operations didn't know that other departments might find it useful.

To fix the problem, the organization asked specific employees in each department to become liaisons. They instituted a weekly meeting at which managers from all departments got together to talk about their work. Each meeting was themed, so lower-level employees whose work related to the theme also were brought into the discussions.

In short, the not-for-profit engineered higher external range into its staff. As a result, operations learned that marketing and PR could make hay out of findings that linked a growing volume of complaints in a specific industry to certain weather patterns and seasons. Because operations employees learned that such insights would be useful, they began to analyze their data in new ways.

Vulnerability

Although having people who can help move information and insights from one part of the organization to another is healthy, an overreliance on those individuals can make a company vulnerable.

Vulnerability Signature

Focus: Organization

Predicts: Which employees the organization can't afford to lose

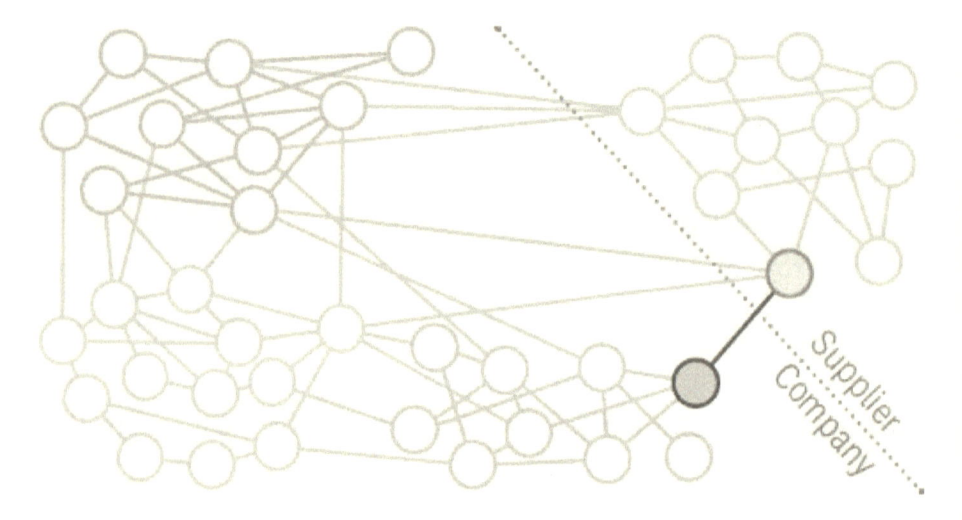

Green is a critical external supplier to company departments blue, purple, and orange. Six people at the company have relationships with green, but 30 people rely on those relationships—which puts the company at risk. If blue's one connection to green leaves, for example, the department will be cut off from the supplier. While his title may not reflect his importance, that employee is vital to information flow.

Take the case of an employee we'll call Arvind, who was a manager in the packaging division at one of the world's top consumer goods companies. He was a connector who bridged several divisions. He talked regularly with counterparts and suppliers across the world. But on the organizational chart, Arvind was nobody special: just a midlevel manager who was good at his job. Companies are at risk of losing employees like Arvind because no obvious attribute signals their importance, so firms don't know what they've got until it's gone.

Without Arvind, the packaging division would lack *robustness*. Networks are robust when connections can be maintained if you remove nodes—employees—from it. In this case, if Arvind left the company, some departments would lose all connection with other departments and with suppliers.

It wasn't that Arvind was irreplaceable. He just wasn't *backed up*. The company didn't realize that no other nodes were making the necessary network connections he provided. That made it vulnerable: If Arvind was out sick or on vacation, work slowed. If Arvind decided that he didn't like one of the suppliers and stopped interacting with it, work slowed. And if Arvind had too much on his plate and couldn't keep up with his many connections, work also slowed.

It wasn't that Arvind was irreplaceable. He just wasn't backed up.

On the day Noshir came to show the company this vulnerability in the packaging division, he entered a boardroom filled with cakes and sweets. A senior executive happily told him that the firm was throwing a party for Arvind. He was retiring. Noshir's jaw dropped. The party went on, but after learning how important Arvind was, the company worked out a deal to retain him for several more years and, in the meantime, used relational analytics to do some succession planning so that multiple people could take on his role.

Capture Your Company's Digital Exhaust - Once you understand the six structural signatures that form the basis of relational analytics, it's relatively easy to act on the insights they provide. Often, the fixes they suggest aren't complex: Set up cross-functional meetings, enable influential people, retain your Arvinds.

Why, then, don't most companies use relational analytics for performance management? There are two reasons. The first is that many network analyses companies do are little more than pretty pictures of nodes and edges. They don't identify the patterns that predict performance.

The second reason is that most organizations don't have information systems in place to capture relational data. But all companies do have a crucial hidden resource: their digital exhaust—the logs, e-trails, and contents of everyday digital activity. Every time employees send one another e-mails in Outlook, message one another on Slack, like posts on Facebook's Workplace, form teams in Microsoft Teams, or assign people to project milestones in Trello, the platforms record the interactions. This information can be used to construct views of employee, team, and organizational networks in which you can pick out the structural signatures we've discussed.

For several years we've been developing a dashboard that captures digital exhaust in real time from these various platforms and uses relational analytics to help managers find the right employees for tasks, staff teams for efficiency and innovation, and identify areas in the organization that are siloed and vulnerable to turnover. Here are some of the things we've learned in the process:

Passive collection is easier on employees. To gather relational data, companies typically survey employees about whom they interact with. Surveys take time, however, and the answers can vary in accuracy (some employees are just guessing). Also, to be truly useful, relational data must come from everyone at the company, not just a few people. As an executive at a large financial services company told us, "If I gave each of my 15,000 employees a survey that takes half an hour to do, we've just lost a million dollars in productivity. And what if their relationships change in a month? Will we have to do it again at a cost of an additional $1 million in people hours?"

Company-collected relational data, however, creates new challenges. Although most employment contracts give firms the right to record and monitor activities conducted on company systems, some employees feel that the passive collection of relational data is an invasion of privacy. This is not a trivial concern. Companies need clear HR policies about the gathering and analysis of digital exhaust that help employees understand and feel comfortable with it.

What About Employee Privacy? Relational analytics changes the equation when it comes to the privacy of employee data. When employees actively provide information about themselves in hiring forms, surveys, and the like, they know their company has and can use it. But they may not even realize that the passive collection of relational data—such as whom they chat with on Slack or when they were copied on email—is happening or that such information is being analyzed.

Job one for companies is to be transparent. If they're going to amass digital exhaust, they should ask employees to sign an agreement indicating they understand that their patterns of interaction on company-owned tools will be tracked for the purposes of analyzing the organization's social networks. Full disclosure with employee consent is the only option.

They have found some additional moves leaders can make to get ahead of privacy concerns: First, give employees whatever relational data you collect about them. We recommend providing it at least annually. The data can include a map of the employee's own network and benchmarks. For example, a report could provide an employee with her constraint score (which shows how inbred someone's social network is) and the average constraint score of employees in her department. That score could then be at the center of a mentoring discussion.

Second, be clear about the depth of relational analytics you intend to invest in. The level that is most basic—and the least prone to privacy concerns—is generic pattern analysis. The analysis might show, for example, that marketing is a silo but not identify specific individuals that contribute to that silo. Or the analysis could show that a certain percentage of teams have the signature for innovation but not identify which teams.

The second level identifies which specific employees in a company have certain kinds of networks. Scores may provide evidencebased predictions about employee behavior—such as who is likely to be an influencer or whose departure would make an organization vulnerable. Although this level of analysis provides more value to the company, it singles particular employees out.

The highest level pairs relational analytics with machine learning. In this scenario, companies collect data about whom employees interact with and about the topics they discuss. Firms examine the content of emails and posts on socialnetworking sites to identify who has expertise in what domains. This information provides the most specific guidance for leaders—for example, about who is likely to develop good ideas in certain areas. This most advanced level obviously also comes with the most privacy concerns, and senior leadership must develop deeply considered strategies to deal with them.

Behavioural data is a better reflection of reality

As we've noted, digital exhaust is less biased than data collected through surveys. For instance, in surveys people may list connections they think they're supposed to interact with, rather than those they actually do interact with. And because every employee will be on at least several communication platforms, companies can map networks representing the entire workforce, which makes the analysis more accurate.

Also, not all behaviors are equal. Liking someone's post is different from working on a team with someone for two years. Copying someone on an e-mail does not indicate a strong relationship. How all those individual behaviors are weighted and combined matters. This is where machine-learning algorithms and simulation models are helpful. With a little technical know-how (and with an understanding of which structural signatures predict what performance outcomes), setting up those systems is not hard to do.

Constant updating is required

Relationships are dynamic. People and projects come and go. To be useful, relational data must be timely. Using digital exhaust in a relational analytics model addresses that need.

Additionally, collecting relational data over time gives analysts more choices about what to examine. For example, if an employee was out on maternity leave for several months, an analyst can exclude that time period from the data or decide to aggregate a larger swath of data. If a company was acquired in a particular year, an analyst can compare relational data from before and after the deal to chart how the company's vulnerabilities may have changed.

Analyses need to be close to decision makers

Most companies rely on data scientists to cull insights related to talent and performance management. That often creates a bottleneck, because there aren't enough data scientists to address all management queries in a timely manner. Plus, data scientists don't know the employees they are running analyses on, so they cannot put results into context.

Dashboards are key

A system that identifies structural signatures and highlights them visually moves analytic insights closer to the managers who need them. As one executive at a semiconductor chip firm told us, "I want my managers to have the data to make good decisions about how to use their employees. And I want them to be able to do it when those decision points happen, not later."

PEOPLE ANALYTICS IS a new way to make evidence-based decisions that improve organizations. But in these early days, most companies have been focused on the attributes of individuals, rather than on their relationships with other employees. Looking at attributes will take firms only so far. If they harness relational analytics, however, they can estimate the likelihood that an employee, a team, or an entire organization will achieve a performance goal. They can also use algorithms to tailor staff assignments to changes in employee networks or to a particular managerial need. The best firms, of course, will use relational analytics to augment their own decision criteria and build healthier, happier, and more-productive organizations.

Leaders to define path...

CHRO plays a vital role in defining leadership of the organization. We may know that leadership defines success or failure of the Organization/functions. The role of CHRO or HR Head is to align functional leadership to Organizational leadership. Many say that organizations fail to achieve its goal or objectives due to business reasons; I say it is because of lack of leadership alignment at leadership/functional levels. Now the question here is how CHRO or HR Head can become a leadership Navigator to the organization.

#Role of HR as future thinker

Vision and foresight are the main traits which distinguish a leader from the led. Leaders possess the capability of developing long-term perspective. They should be able to see clearly ahead through the thick fog of uncertainty and discern as to what lies ahead. Although everybody has the ability to see ahead, the difference is that the leaders are able to get a longer distance and time perspective of the futuristic scenario, and that, too in a sharp focus. CHRO as a leader must be able to visualize what people challenges organization may phase in terms of manpower, compensation, up-skilling, talent management and development, engagements, Organizational changes may be required due to volatility of business and its growth. He should support/guide functional leaders in key hurdles they may face in meeting business goals. It is not only about visualizing but he should translate vision into action. He should support functions to set specific goals that contribute directly to the attainment of the vision. CHRO should encourage organization leaders to think and act in ways that make the vision an eventual reality. He is an conceptual architecture who makes sense out of various aspects and aspirations of the organization's parts. He challenges the best talents of group members by making bold pronouncements about the problems and opportunities in the organization's near term or long-term future.

#Role as Relationship Builder

One of the important attribute of HR Head is having strong inter-personal skills which help to build relationship with cross functions. The leader practices and fosters relationships that help the organization achieve its mission. Especially as leaders mature, their value to organizations may lie primarily in the range and depth of their personal and professional associations. HR Head should assemble and manage teams that make the most of the complementary talents of group members. In order to build a good team spirit he has to build over a period good relations by his deeds. Personnel structures:- The leader establishes the formal relationships among job categories and levels of responsibility within the organization. HR head should build networks that proves valuable to the organization. He should build relations in such a way that he is able to sense odd and evens for the organization from the opinion leaders and make necessary strategies for the organization.

As an Influencer

CHRO plays a vital role as an influencer in the organization. He should be capable enough to encourage employees to enhance productivity by positive engagement and motivation. A few years back the role of HR was more of a controller role like managing compliances, ensure policies and procedures are maintained well, HR administration etc. Today his role has changed drastically, he is today a Chief change officer as mentioned earlier, he is a solution finder for present and future people related problems in business. He encourages decision making by effectively managing the nature and frequency of decision –making, he also determines what degree others will be involved in decision-making process. He influences effective delegation of the organization and functions so that the goal of the organization is achieved. He influences CEO and Board for taking corrective measures on organization people strategies dealing with compensations, manpower planning and other key people imperatives. You must have seen in organization that it is not easy to influence or implement an opinion/policy/a unpleasant message etc. I have seen many organizations have employees who are good at influencing …I call them as **"Opinion Leaders"** this people play a vital role in communicating message to the organization and also find out the grapevine going on within organization and also what employee are wanting or looking forward. This actually helps a lot to leaders to redraft or formulate the communication well proof before they are out in the organization. This leaders are real influencers, they have this in them as a quality. HR Heads should make use of them very well.

#The Encouragement Role...

A leaders role is also to encourage people to do things when the situation are uncertain. HR head should try to develop a culture or environment which encourages people to take risk, fail but still do not stop doing things which they are good with. A healthy and a successful organization is one which encourages employees to experiment without any inhibition, that way the brains are agile and innovation are born. HR Heads/Leaders should come up with encouraging ideas which can help build employee morale and motivation which will definitely result for better productivity. Let me tell you a story about Ben & Jerry......... Ben Cohen and Jerry Greenfield founder of Ben and Jerry's Ice Cream were excellent leaders and always passionate about doing things which inspired them. While they had completion who was doing every thing to bring them down, but these guys were clear what they were for. Jerry, with a sharp intuition for people's concerns, had noticed at one point that some of the production people were becoming complacent and the general cheerfulness level was dropping. His solution was the "Joy Gang." He posted a notice in the Waterbury plant asking that any employee who wanted to help him boost morale to contact him. The " Joy Gang" then met twice a month to initiate ideas that would make working in the plant more fun. Some of the good ideas that had been implemented were a stereo system for the production floor, a hot chocolate machine in the freezer, and a weekly visit from a massage therapist. Jerry also ensured that the employees were allowed to eat as much ice cream as they wanted while working on the production line. All employees were allowed to take home up to three pints of ice cream per day. These actions of the employer encouraged employees so well that they started giving extra time for better productivity and finally better business results.

#The Information Role...

It is tactics that HR Heads should apply when it comes to communication or information role leader. He should what to communicate and when to communicate and what impact that will make to the organization. As mentioned earlier on opinion leader, The HR Head should maintain internal and external communication channels. The information role consists of the following five categories. **Design Information** – The leader oversees the design and maintenance of an information system that serves, the needs of the organization in attaining its mission. **Monitoring** – The leader keeps a finger on the pulse of important information sources for early warning of problems and occasions to seize opportunities. **Informing** –The leader provides stakeholders in the organization with the information they need to best serve the organization's interest. **Consulting** – The leader seeks out expert counsel inside and outside the organization. **Mentoring**- The leader encourages learning at all levels with the organization.

Role as High Performance enhancing Navigator

Every human organization creates a unique culture all its own. From a small family business operating in its hometown, to a large global corporation spanning national cultures and time zones, each organization has a distinct identity. Tribes, families, cults, teams and corporations all develop a complex and unique identity that evolves as they grow through the years. Their culture always reflects the collective wisdom that comes from the lessons people learn as they adapt and survive together over time.

Research over the past two or three decades has shown that an organization's culture has an impact on business performance in four main ways.

- Creating an organization's sense of *mission* and direction

- Building a high level of *adaptability* and flexibility
- Nurturing the *involvement* and engagement of their people
- Providing a *consistency* that is strongly rooted in a set of core values.

These are the cultural traits that most clearly affect business performance, so this is where the journey must begin.

Mission – Successful organizations have a clear sense of purpose and direction that allows them to define organizational goals and strategies and to create a compelling vision of the organization's future. Leaders play a critical role in defining mission, but a mission can only be reached if it is well understood, top to bottom. A clear mission provides purpose and meaning by defining a compelling social role and a set of goals for the organization. We focus on three aspects of mission: strategic direction and intent, goals and objectives and vision.

Adaptability – A strong sense of purpose and direction must be complemented by a high degree of flexibility and responsiveness to the business environment. Organizations with a strong sense of purpose and direction often are the least adaptive and the most difficult to change. Adaptable organizations, in contrast, quickly translate the demands of the organizational environment into action. We focus on three dimensions of adaptability: creating change, customer focus and organizational learning.

Involvement- Effective organizations empower and engage their people, build their organization around teams, and develop human capability at all levels. Organizational members are highly committed to their work and feel a strong sense of engagement and ownership. People at all levels feel that they have input into the decisions that affect their work and feel that their work is directly connected to the goals of the organization. We focus on three characteristics of involvement: empowerment, team orientation, and capability development.

Consistency- Organizations are most effective when they are consistent and well integrated. Behavior must be rooted in a set of core values, and people must be skilled at putting these values into action by reaching agreement while incorporating diverse points of view. These organizations have highly committed employees, a distinct method of doing business, a tendency to promote from within, and a clear set of do's and don'ts. This type of consistency is a powerful source of stability and internal integration. We focus on three consistency factors: core values, agreement and coordination and integration.

IKEA: Mission Grows Out of Core Beliefs and Assumptions...... IKEA founder Ingwar Kamprad grew up in the hardscrabble farmlands of southern Sweden and became an entrepreneur at an early age. By 1976, well established in the Swedish furniture business, he summarized his key principles of doing business in a little book called A *Furniture Dealer's Testament* it is remarkable how many of the principles described in this book are still alive at IKEA over forty years later. Like most great organizations, Kamprad's company has not just produced profits but has also tried to serve a higher purpose in the world. IKEA brings style, value and a better life to many. The company's products are designed for the global everyman, combining frugality, innovation, and style, using environmentally friendly materials. Everyone deserves the opportunity to be part of the IKEA revolution. Kamprad also expressed strong beliefs about how IKEA should operate; stressing the simplicity and self-reliance of an individual who today is worth over $41 billion but still counts every penny like it was his last. Consider his thoughts on simplicity: **Bureaucracy complicates and paralyzes! Exaggerated planning is the most common cause of corporate death. We do not need fancy cars, posh titles, tailor-made uniforms or other status symbols. We rely on our strength and our will.**

IKEA is a terrific example of how a global business strategy can grow from the core beliefs and assumptions of the founders. Consider just one key elements IKEA system: the *flatpack*. As all loyal IKEA shoppers know, after following the one way corridor through the store, looking at the kitchens and the bedrooms, and stopping at the restaurant for a coffee or light meal, you eventually make your way to checkout and finally pick up your purchases. They are all packed in flat boxes designed to take home and assemble yourself. Where did this brilliant strategic innovation come from? Was it the result of an expensive study from a leading consultancy? Or an outgrowth of a corporate innovation center designed to make IKEA more customer centric? No way! In 1952, one of IKEA's first employee, Gillis Lundgren, had a problem. He was trying to load a table into his Volvo to deliver to a customer. It didn't fit. Gillis thought, "God, what a lot of space that takes up! Let's take the legs off and put them under the table top. The rest is just implementation. By 1956, this practice was standardized and has been essential part of the IKEA experience ever since. The current system has continued to build on these key principles established in the early days.

Ritz-Carlton Hotels: Involvement Creates Capacity...... Ritz-Cazlton hotel founder Cesar Ritz set the luxury standard for European Hotels in the early twentieth century. He said "Never say no when a client asks for something, even if they ask for the moon. Ritz- Carlton's three steps of service set a high standard for five –star quality:

1. A war and sincere greeting. Use the guest's name
2. Anticipation and fulfillment of each quest's needs.
3. A fond farewell. Give a warm good-bye use the guest's name.

The Ritz-Carlton refers to their twenty-eight thousand people as "ladies and gentleman, serving ladies and gentleman" Their remarkable core values are well understood by their people, starting with the "Employee Promise "and the Credo. But perhaps the most remarkable part of all of this is what it takes to actually do this: every day, all of the Ritz-Carlton ladies and gentlemen participates in a daily briefing. All of their service people, in all their hotels, meet to discuss the incidents that arose through the day, the actions that they took to address them, and how those fit with the Ritz-Carlton principles. This debrief is led by the local manager. The day's incidents and actions are also captured in their system so that they have a record of every guest's experience in each stay. That record can be used to anticipate and accommodate a guest's experience, even if it is at any other Ritz-Carlton Hotel. This allows the staff to achieve an unusual mark of distinction: they can create the same level of customer service for each of their clients at each hotel. The staff of Ritz-Carlton the ladies and gentleman in their service operations has the authority to spend $2500 on the spot to resolve a guest's concerns. But the key is the daily debrief...without which Ritz wouldn't have been what it is today.

So to conclude chapter three that is... **HR doesn't understand business expectations and doesn't deliver as per management needs...**It is not true that Human resources do not understand the needs of the organization, what they have to learn is how to identify challenges and define business oriented solutions which can contribute to effective growth of the organization.

Outsiders promises you things even before they know you

4

Where Should We Head To?

The concluding chapter is about understanding where should the HR function or people function or CHRO/Leaders head to. There are four important aspects of management I would like to portray in this chapter

1. A world of Trust and Being Human
2. New Dimension
3. I Will Get There?
4. Way To Growth?

A World of Trust and Being Human

As we all know business runs on "Trust" however I feel these days the trust word has been missing in the corporates or may be in business. We all are so busy pushing targets that sometime we forget the essence of doing business which may be much bigger reason then just making money. Today you see in Covid19 situation money is not helping you, whether you are rich or poor you don't have a choice but to stay at home under lock down or quarantined. All are fighting and struggling to push away covid.

In December 2019 I was in Himachal for a vacation with my wife and few friends. While exploring few exciting tourist spots, we went to see a place from where people try paragliding. There was a small tea shop where we wanted to have some hot Maggie and some tea. I asked him whether he had enough Maggie as we were 4 of us and every one was hungry to have at least two packets of Maggie. He said "Ho jayaga Shaab" then he told me "shaab I'm all alone in the shop, can you guard my shop for sometime I will get Maggie and water for making Maggie and tea". I was thinking Maggie fine he may get it from somewhere else, but water from where he is getting? That was bit worry for me. Anyway I said ok no problem, but how long as we had to head to a different place. He said just few minutes, he went to a shop nearby and got Maggie, and then you will not believe he went down the hill for a while to get water from the stream, which was more pure than your mineral water which you buy in shop. He took all the pain to go down the hill to serve us the best Maggie made out of stream water (I believe Maggi made out of stream water tastes better – That is the logic he gave me). We really relished the hot Maggie in such a lovely chilled weather …You know how it is in Dec in Hill stations. We ate almost 2 packets each and hot tea was awesome! I asked him how much to pay he said X amount, but I immediately realized I was out of cash and was carrying only cards, checked with my wife she had left her bag in friends place where we stayed. My friends also didn't have cash as we forgot to stop in ATM and withdraw cash. This was very embarrassing situation for us particularly for me. I told him we don't have cash right now, we have cards and we can't expect you to have card machine in between of nothing. What I can do is go down and get cash which will take at least 2 to 3 hours, hope that is fine with you or you can keep my watch instead as assurance. He smiled at me and said Shaabji why are you so worried, you all head to your destination where you have planned to go, you can give me whenever you are coming next. Infact he insisted us to go ahead with our plans. I felt bad for such a foolish thing of mine. That day evening it started raining heavily and we were all informed about landslide which happened in Hills above and hence I couldn't go up to pay him. It took almost 3 days to clear the landslide and open the road. On 5th day I went up and paid him the money, he never said anything he only said please come again, it was pleasure meeting you.

We speak about Trust and some people like the tea shopkeeper demonstrate the same. Similarly the Organization/Employer should demonstrate trust in the organization in the manner mentioned below, that will make a high productive organization.

Now the question is how do we go back to the world of trust and belief? When we look at Trust per say I look at four important aspects to discuss.

How can we be a credible organization

Credibility or the belief that your organization can do what it promises, builds trust, which feeds into building your brand's reputation and cementing customer or client loyalty. Remember that people do business with those they trust and like. Organizations should make it clear to employees through continuous communication what it can do and what I cannot do. Companies should not make employees build up on expectations, that will create un- expected problem. We as management people are not so good in giving feedbacks and communicating clearly the expectations or what organizations can offer in terms of any personal developments or compensation and benefits and other things. Few ways by which companies can build credibility

Hear out: - My Mother use to always say you only hear 25% to 50% of what is say, and this became true for many years. In organizations we hear less and act more on communication without analysing the impact in most of the times. At work, tuning people out can be dangerous, especially when you're managing them. You might miss important feedback, directions, or updates. Even worse? If your team thinks you're not hearing them, they won't confide in you. That can diminish the chances that they'll turn to you when they have questions or need help, which in turn prevents them from producing their best work.

That's why it's so important to learn how to actively listen, especially in the early stages of building credibility and earning trust as a leader. It's not an easy task at first -- especially when we're constantly overloaded with information and stimuli -- but it can be learned with a few good habits. When colleagues are speaking to you, keep distractions minimized or at bay; try moving the conversation away from anything that might cause your attention to stray, like your computer or mobile devices. And don't be afraid to do whatever's necessary to make sure you heard the person correctly, even if it means repeating back to them what you think you heard.

Don't beat around the Bush.: As mentioned in my early chapters also don't beat around the bush get to the point. As a leader you should always try to get into the point instead of spending time talking about irrelevant things. Don't take it for granted about Millennial or people in today's era, most of them are well read or are aware of things (Thanks to Google search) they know or atleast understand why are they called for or may sense so.So when you speak to your team, cut to the chase -- you want them to remember the important parts. You have to be clear, simple and properly expressed manner called as succinctly in your communication. The first, "clearly," is particularly important -- according to a recent Wrike work management survey, 37% of employees blamed "unclear priorities" for decreased productivity. So don't water down your message with a lot of big words or details to prove your competence; not only does that detract from your confidence as a leader, which we'll get to later, but it'll undercut focus from your main takeaways.

Acting the same way:- Consistency proves a leader. Let me give you an example well know food company, they are market leaders in Ready to Eat packets which was a famous packed food products for Indians travelling abroad. The market was going through ups and downs due to new companies getting into this business, so this company thought that they will come up with a different packaging system to attract millennial customers and for those who frequently travel. They changed the earlier packaging of normal flat packets to tray shaped packets as an initiative of new product development. The organization was expecting good sale as they were sure this will work for the consumers. But somehow the new innovation back fired as consumers were always happy carrying flat packs as that were easily fitting in the suitcase. Realizing the facts the company had to withdraw the new packs and got back to the old packaging. This is what called as consumer consistency they always like the product and its packaging and never wanted a change.

One of my know person a senior industrialist said something that really resonated with me. "Do what you say you'll do." It seems simple in theory, right? But imagine this scenario: Being goal-oriented, you've taught yourself to eradicate the word "no" from your vocabulary. So you start off by saying "yes" to everything -- more than any one person can actually take on -- until you realize you've completely over-committed and can't deliver on everything you agreed to. Been there? I have. If you go from always saying "yes" to being so overwhelmed with commitments that you snap at new requests, it creates a major inconsistency in your leadership style. It makes your temperament look unpredictable, which can really stress out your team and make people less inclined to approach you. In fact, a recent study showed that employees actually prefer a manager who's consistently mean over one with erratic behaviour. "One of the most important things for leaders to think about is consistency," James Harder, Director of Communications at Morgan Memorial Goodwill Industries, told "If your messaging is consistent, it gives you more credibility. That is true with any phase of marketing, or for that matter, communication." So before you make a promise, be sure to ask yourself, "Is this a priority? Can I really take this on right now?" Knowing when to say "no" will create a balanced sense of priority among your team, and on your own to-do list.

Transparency. Once I remember having a conversation with a SVP of HR. I no longer recall the exact details we were discussing but I clearly recall his attitude. "You can't tell employees that - that stuff is dynamite." Yep, "dynamite" was the word used. It's that kind of non-transparent thinking, treating employees as lesser beings incapable of understanding facts, that undermines credibility. This HR approach ignored two fundamental things: Plenty of employees are every bit as intelligent as their management and they spend a lot of time observing their management closely. Transparency matters, and there's ample research supporting it. Want credibility? You've got to be straight with people or you'll always be bucking the current, a trout swimming upstream.

Recognition:- You have get to know as many people as possible... when asked a Harvard Business School Leadership professor for his thoughts on leadership credibility, he summed it up with one line: It's "built by doing, enabling, and recognizing great work." So while you're likely in a position of leadership because of your own achievements, it's important to acknowledge that people around you do good work, too.

Why is that? Well, to start, employee recognition goes a long way -- 70% of employees in North America say that receiving recognition is "effective," for example, when it comes to their engagement. But by going beyond the parameters of your own team, you're better able to recognize the far-reaching talent throughout your organization. Reaching out to more people within your organization sends the message that you're open to different perspectives. Since that kind of behaviour shows that you're looking beyond your own self-interest, it can build credibility.

At HubSpot, for example, we follow the philosophy of solving for the customer first. So when our leaders are able to seek out multiple perspectives and talents within the company, it ultimately leads to more people improving and creating new solutions.

Lead by example. Again, this is basic but it's often ignored and there's no good alternative to it. If you don't lead by example - if you "talk the walk but don't walk the talk" - you'll alienate more than motivate. As I noted earlier, employees watch their management closely. If they conclude management is playing by its own set of rules, it kills credibility. If they conclude management is "more Catholic than the Pope" (as the saying goes), it builds credibility. Coming back to Mr. Covey's initial point about the "speed of trust," he liked to tell the story of a major acquisition that Warren Buffett's company, Berkshire Hathaway, once made from Walmart. It was a $23 billion deal and under normal circumstances would have taken many months of serious mistrustful haggling. But in this instance, since both organizations were operating from a position of high credibility, the deal "was made with one two-hour meeting and a handshake," Covey wrote. "In less than a month, it was completed. High trust, high speed, low cost." Always an invaluable leadership asset, credibility can do that for you.

Leaders go out of their way to find speaking opportunities. "Not only will it get your name out there," which is always a good way to build credibility, but "it'll give you good practice. The more advanced you become in your career, the more you will be expected to speak." Speaking makes you connect well with people around. People need to hear you more to understand your credibility.

How do develop an environment of respect

The respect dimension measures the extent to which employees feel respected by management by assessing the levels of support, collaboration, and caring employees see expressed through management's actions toward them. There are people who believe respect is given and some believe respect is earned. While the latter is true, but we cannot ignore the fact that...respect has to be given.

Give Respect:- I have seen in many cases the one and only reasons for employees to leave the organization is because he/she felt were not treated well by their Manager. We all know employees leave managers not companies. It is not the high salary or high perks or job promotions are important as respect is! If you are not treated well with respect, the employee will be a short term resource for you. They say an employee makes up in his mind within 15 days of his joining how long he is going to work for this organization. So your first 15 days of employee joining is very important to treat him in a manner he wants to be treated. Employee are hungry of being given the respect they deserve during his/her stay in the Organization.

DHL was always considered as a people oriented organization. Seema was a very hard and smart Customer service executive in DHL Calcutta. Because of her hardwork and dedication she was transferred to Mumbai head office for DHL India. She was promoted as Assistant Manager Customer service in her new job. A born Bengali Seema was used to Bengali festivals and other cultural events in Calcutta, so many a times she used to miss those occasions. But she never cribbed or complained, she was such a dedicated and good customer support manager that apart from the office colleagues and her manager the customers also would like her work ethics and approach very much. Because of her good work she became a blue eyed girl of her Operations Customer service Head, Francis. One day during the month of Oct, few days before the great Durga Puja (Durga puja is the greatest festival for Bengalis, where everyone in the family is expected to be together and celebrate, in fact Durga Puja is celebrated in such a large scale in Bengal that it is considered as one of biggest festival in India) day Francis saw her bit upset and kind of bit lost. Francis understood the reason, without talking to her he went back to his cabin. After 2 days, Francis called Seema to his cabin, Seema was bit worried, whether she has done any mistake unknowingly. Francis made her sit and gave her an envelope, she opened it and found 2 tickets to and fro to Kolkata, she was shocked/surprised, before she could say anything, Francis said Seema please go and enjoy your Durga Puja. She was trilled and cried out of joy. This is respect she got as being a good employee. Everyone looks for appreciation in a manner which can boost their self-esteem that is when he/she is being respected.

Earn Respect:- Earning respect is right of every individual, they have work towards earning respect, when they see they are not getting into when they are supposed to get. Difficult to earn and easily lost, trust and respect are two of the most important characteristics of great leadership. Workers look to their leaders for guidance and behavioral cues that influence the way they react to a given situation. So, the trust a workforce has for the people in charge greatly impacts productivity. For a HR head or a leader it is important to earn respect by setting examples, walking the talk, being transparent, Get your hands dirty, confidence in your decision, share your wisdom

Setting examples:- If you have to earn respect with people and employees you have set examples by doing things which they get influenced and try to practice in their day to day work.

Walk the talk:- Leaders should commit only when they are sure, don't over committee and then fail. That will be a deterrent to earning respect. Be clear in what have to be achieved and then plan well before you communicate to the team or employees.

Being Transparent:- Don't work in silence. I get it, you're used to the college way of working where you get an assignment, and hand it in when it's done as you work on it on your own time. It's easy to get assignments and work on it in your silo until it's complete, or simply execute on a task without circling back to say that it's done (since you're likely thinking oh, my boss will see that it's done). This is wrong. Your boss or colleagues shouldn't have to check to see if something is complete, they should be notified by you directly with a link to the work, a screenshot or attachment of the task. This shows you are on top of your stuff, and that you're thorough. Humble yourself, learn as much as you can about your industry and your craft, and continue to network inside and outside of the office to set a strong foundation for your career.

Get your hands dirty:- There are few better ways to build respect than rolling up your sleeves and jumping down into the trenches with your employees. Showing that you aren't afraid to step out on the front line and get your hands dirty creates a bond through shared experience and reminds your workers that you've been there and have personally walked a few miles in their shoes.

Confidence in your decisions:- Mental fortitude and resoluteness create confidence among the people you lead that they are following the right person. Wishy-washy decision making and uncertainty when the going gets tough causes doubt, and when the team isn't fully behind their leader, a breakdown in communication and productivity is sure to follow.

Share your wisdom:- As iron sharpens iron, one person sharpens another—leaders who give willingly of their time and expertise to build up the next generation earn trust and respect from the people they lead. Not only do they set the standard for future leadership, they also leave behind a legacy worth celebrating. Workforce productivity and success hinges largely on examples set by the people at the top. Building trust doesn't happen overnight, but the leaders who invest the time to foster a positive working environment based on mutual respect will be rewarded with employees who are more engaged and loyal to their company.

Being Fair

Being fair defines the culture of the organization. Fairness is being equitable or honest, it also refers to organizational justice. Justice as a social phenomenon has received a great deal of research attention from social psychologists. With new research on fairness in organizations, scholars in organizational behaviour, industrial/organizational psychology, and managers are provided with practical orientations on how to create fair working environments. Although organizational justice is not a panacea for managers, it can help boost employee morale and cooperation. Perceptions of unfairness have been related to several negative reactions such as employee theft, lack of commitment, lawsuits, and recently aggressive behaviours in the workplace. Perceptions of fair treatment, on the other hand, have been related to attitudinal and behavioural outcomes such as employee commitment, trust, and cooperation that are conducive to organizational performance. The most important asset of any organization is its workforce and the way people are treated shapes attitudes and behaviours such as commitment, trust, performance, turnover, aggression, and all issues of human resources. As we are moving toward a more educated workforce, people want not only better jobs but also to be treated with respect and dignity in the workplace. We are entering an era in which issues of fairness in a diversity of forms will be high on the agenda of corporate management, thus a better understanding of issues of justice in modern organizations is imperative for human resource managers. How many times have you heard someone say, "That's not fair"? If you're a parent, then probably more times than you can count. If you're a business leader, then probably only slightly fewer times.

Employee concerns over pay systems, managerial favouritism and equal recognition are common leadership challenges. While leaders of some of the best small workplaces struggle with fairness issues just like their corporate counterparts, we've found that they often achieve more favourable results among their staffs nearly 10 percent more often. This greater success is the result of thoughtful and comprehensive management approaches. To help your organization strengthen its own tactics, here are a few lessons to consider:

Reaffirm that everyone will receive an equal opportunity to be recognized. One of the fastest ways to erode a workplace's sense of fairness is by giving recognition unequally. This challenge can be especially difficult when managing employees across multiple sites. When McMurry, a Phoenix, Ariz.-based full-service marketing communications company, acquired a second site, leaders were faced with how to adapt their annual employee awards event in order to promote fairness. The company's leaders doubled up, dividing the event into two presentations -- one at each site held in successive weeks. The events were coordinated so that when one location held its event, a simultaneous celebration was held in the other.

Being fair is not only having fair policies in the organization, about promotions or rewards, but respecting fairness. While many companies have fairness as a part of their Human resources policies, preaching and practicing fairness defines the richness of culture of the organization. Let me give you a sports example. When Pierre de Coubertin revived the Modern Olympics, he set out to accomplish many goals – one of which was to bring the world together to compete in sport in "a spirit of Fair Play". Fair Play is a virtue of rule adherence whereby players and athletes abide by the rules of competition. It is also a commitment to contest in a good spirit and encourages a good attitude towards sport that includes respect, modesty, generosity and friendship. Since Coubertin's time, the Olympic Games have encountered more challenges to Fair Play than perhaps at first imagined. It is now more important than ever to educate players and athletes in the principles of Fair Play and to spread its lessons not only within the sporting world – but everywhere.

This unit Fair Play, explores the history of Fair Play as it relates to sport and the Olympic Movement and looks at Fair Play as an essential component of both sport and life. The term "Fair Play" covers both observing the rules and behaving in a sporting spirit. It demonstrates attitudes and behaviours in sport consistent with the belief that sport is an ethical pursuit. It does not include acts of violence, cheating, drug abuse or any form of exploitation in an effort to win.

Create a sense that promotions are handled fairly. When an employee complains that a co-worker's promotion wasn't fair, his or her underlying question might actually be, "Why wasn't I promoted?" The best organizations address this by ensuring all employees receive frequent, constructive feedback and by providing personal support in professional development. Employees at Ehrhardt Keefe Steiner & Hottman, a Denver-based accounting firm, receive feedback at least once every month, if not at the end of every client engagement. To ensure this experience feels balanced, employees also have the opportunity to give upward feedback to their manager on the client engagement. In addition, all of the firm's professionals have a coach that is typically a level above them. Coaches meet regularly with their advisees to provide one-on-one feedback and discuss what issues and goals the advisee may have. These coaches also partner with employees to develop personal and professional development goals with action steps to achieve them.

Add transparency and a commitment to equity to the paycheck. When it comes to a sense of fair pay, it's not just about the amount of the paycheck that matters. The transparency of the compensation system and a clear commitment to equity by the organization are critical in ensuring people feel fairly paid. To create transparency, the human-resources department at Johnson & Johnson, a 125-person insurance company based in Charleston, S.C., constructs a total compensation document, known as "Investment Statements," for each employee annually. These documents communicate each employee's total compensation, including items such as base salary, bonus, medical coverage, paid time off and several other factors.

Partners at Tucson, Ariz.-based accounting firm Heinfeld, Meech & Co. meet annually for a daylong process of reviewing a detailed list of all salaries and proposed raises and bonuses for all of the company's 85 employees. After making sure salaries are fair compared to industry and geographical benchmarks, the partners make changes to individual employee's salaries and bonuses to ensure internal fairness between offices and job roles.

Offer a fair appeals process. It is critical for employees to understand that they have a fair opportunity to have grievances heard by management. Parkway Properties, a Jackson, Miss.-based commercial real estate services firm, offers what it calls an Employee Advocate program. Complemented by an open door policy for all leaders and several upward feedback mechanisms, this program allows team members the opportunity to voice concerns or constructive criticisms to an employee outside of his or her regular communication channel. These questions are directed to the company's executive officers and are shared only with them, the senior vice president of the "People Department" and the chief executive. Then, "Employee Advocates" schedule regular visits at each of the company's locations, ensuring team members have reliable opportunities to air a grievance. Workplace concerns about fairness are challenging for any business and can be frustrating for employees and leaders alike. Focusing on transparency and frequent communication can cut down these concerns, allowing everyone to focus on more rewarding and productive responsibilities.

Delight and Fulfilment

What I believe is customer delight can only happen when your internal customer is delighted. I mean your employees of the organization are delighted. It is just like preparing a nice Pizza without cheese. The customer delights comes only when the customer realizes the cheese spread done well in the Pizza. Employee delight helps employees to perform better, employees get empowered by being accountable and responsible. Clear about organizational goals and expectations from them. Employee Delight will make employee develop new skills and competencies required for future development which will result in customer satisfaction and retention. It integrates the organizational culture with the employees personal and professional needs. It helps in cross functional teaming, which results in achieving organizational goals, rather than only individual KPI achievement or functional objectives. Let me quote an example of employee delight which lead to customer delight.

Aparna was a very delighted employee of DHL India. Based at Kolkata eastern regional office, she was associated with DHL as Customer service executive. Aparna was a smart and committed lady and new her job very well. She was delighted because DHL gave her the right platform to perform better, she liked the culture of the organization of common business language spoke all over DHL, she was frequently trained to up-skill herself so as to face challenges of customers, she was also given free hand to deliver the best customer service. Always appreciated and recognised for her good work, good support she used to get for her work. She being a contented employee in DHL India always had passion in her to deliver the best. One such incident is mentioned below

Haldia petrochemicals a well know public sector, used to ship all their important documents/shipments through DHL. One day in mid May 2000, Haldia factory had to send important Annual audit documents to Prime Minister's Office, the documents were despatched by DHL to Kolkata Airport to be sent to New Delhi and just when the documents were loaded into the plane, Aparna gets a call from Haldia

Petrochemical office that the document send is incorrect it has to be stopped from despatching, they also said the corrected one had to be despatched back within 24 hours. Aparna tried her best to stop that plane to get the document out, but once cargo/courier is loaded in the plane, it cannot be taken back, and also the plane was about to take off. Now Aparna was desperately waiting when the plane reaches Delhi and she can then stop the courier to be sent ahead. Meanwhile she did all the ground work coordinating with DHL New Delhi office to make sure the document is not missed out for despatch. After few hours when the document reached New Dehli airport she made sure that the document was collected and send to Kolkata by next flight. By end of the day the document was received by Haldia Petrochemicals, they corrected the mistakes in audit document. Meanwhile Aparna had her person ready in Haldia Petrochemical office to collect the document and straight take it to Kolkata airport. The document finally reached the destination well in time. Few days after Haldia Petrochemical Senior Manager came personally to thank her, appreciated with card and sweets for her good job on handling the entire episode on time without any hurdle.

In most of the cases this is possible when the employee is a delighted employee of the organization. Vineet Nayar, former Chief Executive Officer of HCL Technologies in TEDxAix talk spoke about his book "Employee First Customer second" He says every Organization wants to give an unique experience & unique values for their customers, but where does this unique value get created and who creates it? Answer is it gets created where our customers and employees meet. In that interface we call that as value zone and our employees in that value zone create that unique experience. If our employees creates that unique value then what should the role of Managers/Management be? The answer is the role of them is to enable, encourage, inspire, and motivate employees to create that unique experience so that we can go faster. I have seen in my experiences that, it is not the money which bring employee delight. It is the respect, caring, encouraging and appreciating for good job brings customer delights apart from benefits of the organization which has less role to play than being recognized. Whether you are a trainee or a senior employee everyone needs to feel delighted to make customers delighted.

Companionship

We all need friends at work. We spend most of our time atleast in week days in office working, so it is very necessary for us to have friends in the organization, who can guide us and help us in doing our job better. Organizations should encourage employees to develop friends in the organization it serves many purpose few are...Friends @ work helps develop a feel of belongingness, friends @ work helps to create secure and safe environment for employees, friends @ work helps employees to settle down well in organization, friends @ work helps works as a bumping box/Sounding board when they are frustrated, friends @ work helps to develop employee engagement

Employees report that when they have friends at work, their job is more fun, enjoyable, worthwhile, and satisfying. Gallup found that close work friendships boost employee satisfaction by 50% and people with a best friend at work are seven times more likely to engage fully in their work. Camaraderie is more than just having fun, though. It is also about creating a common sense of purpose and the mentality that we are in-it together. Studies have shown that soldiers form strong bonds during missions in part because they believe in the purpose of the mission, rely on each other, and share the good and the bad as a team. In short, camaraderie promotes a group loyalty that result in a shared commitment to and discipline toward the work. Camaraderie at work can create "**esprit de corps**," which includes mutual respect, sense of identity, and admiration to push for hard work and outcomes.

Many companies are engaging in corporate challenges, such as bike to work day, wellness competitions, community service events, and other activities to help build a sense of teamwork and togetherness. Best practice companies also communicate widely about corporate goals and priorities to unify everyone.

Friends at work also form a strong social support network for each other, both personally and professionally. Whether rooting for each other on promotions, consoling each other about mistakes, giving advice, or providing support for personal situations, comradeship at work can boost an employee's spirit and provide needed assistance. A recent story in the Fairfield County Gazette in Ohio highlighted the power of workplace friendship for brain cancer patient Tracy Lee. Three nights a week, one of Tracy's co-workers from the Fairfield County Board of Developmental Disabilities stops by with dinner for the family. Notes containing loving messages such as 'miss your smiley face' cover her office door. This type of support also creates a strong sense of community within the organization.

Some companies — among them Google, DaVita, Dropbox, and Southwest — have built reputations for fostering comradeship at work. Creating comradeship at work hinges on the leaders of organizations. That is, companies can and should create and value camaraderie as a competitive advantage for recruiting top employees, retaining employees, and improving engagement, creativity, and productivity.

How can a leader help foster a culture of camaraderie. First, It is important for the leaders of the organization to have a vision for the culture. You should be clear in your mind on what you want the culture to be within your organization. Many companies have a culture where employees feel they are part of a family. leaders must "model the culture: spending time with employees, treating people with respect, having fun, being there for them personally and professionally, and putting people first — with empathy, kindness and compassion." It is very important for organizations to have products and services around which employees can feel proud and that organizations need to leverage the talents of the employees by letting ideas come forward. People in organizations need to work together. So, managers and employees need to foster collaboration, trust, personal relationships, fun, and support. In an increasingly global and virtual environment, challenges for employees and managers will be to cultivate these personal relationships. Fostering friendships takes proactive effort.

Are there downsides to friendships at work? Sure, there can be bumps: professional jealousy, groupthink, negative cliques, split loyalties, loss of work time to socializing, and broken friendships. However, these are all manageable and the benefits of positive relationships far outweigh any negative outcomes.

Being Human...

People say when you are in office, you were a mask because you need to please bosses, handle politics, and be tactical in your speech and actions. Today the world has both for employer and employee it has become certain that they believe in being human and treat people like a Human. As we all know, once when Alexander the great asked King Porus when he was captured in The Battle of the Hydaspes fought in 326BC. Alexander asked Porus how would he liked to be treated he said "Just like one King treats another King" Now this stands well for Organization as well.

If the organization follows all the above mentioned Trust factors like Credibility, Respect for others, Being Fair, Employee Delight and companionship the Organization is considered to be an organization where they value people and are Being Human. Organization should realize that getting work done is much easier by treating people well and that will motivate employees to perform better.

Many jobs aren't designed with humans' needs in mind. Humans can do them, but they get sick and unhappy. So how do we design jobs that humans enjoy and that keep them healthy and vital? For example, we want to see our children, spend time with our friends, and take time off to regain energy. How do we encourage flexible working and make it work? Encouraging men to take paternity leave is a big issue: If you are going to live for 100 years – which is increasingly likely – and you're only going to have two children, wouldn't it make sense to spend some time with them? Tackling that sort of issue is crucial.

There will always be some human skills that no machine can replicate, like intuition, empathy, complex collaboration and creativity. Good customer service can only be provided by a human – no machine in the world can recognize what is happening to someone's face or voice as well as a person can.

Organizations today are being faced with unprecedented complexity, driven by forces such as competition, globalization and technology. With these conditions comes the need to be agile, or be able to adapt and flourish in changing circumstances. Every organization is calling for greater levels of agility in the face of this complexity. However, we have to recognize that organizations themselves can never be truly agile unless the people who work within them are agile – and more specifically, emotionally agile. This is only possible when you know what you need to motivate them to treat them well so they can contribute without any inhibition.

We always think of cost when we design any developmental areas/benefits/policies for employees. Yes it is important, but don't you think that investment you are making today will rep benefit tomorrow. I think leaders should slowly start thinking differently and consider things which they have not considered.

Being Human make yourself a person of trust and a better leader.

New Dimension... The world is changing...

We should now start looking at Human Capital function bit differently. What we have been doing earlier, will be of less relevant going ahead. New thoughts, new way of working will have to be created. Today Leaders have to develop great sense of innovation and speed decision making capabilities. Because millennial today don't have time to sit and wait, they want decisions now, or else they find ways out. As said earlier also, my request to all leaders is you can only influence things when you start looking at challenges at 360 degree mode, then you may feel the challenge is not a challenge rather a path to solutions.

Few days back I was reading an Article of People Matters...It says Since 2017, Cognizant has been releasing annual reports on the future of jobs, providing data-driven insights into what the world of work will look like for a broad cross-section of industries in the decades to come. Now, the Cognizant Centre for the Future of Work – along with the Future Workplace and its network of leading CHROs – have combined their knowledge to put together their list of 21 HR Jobs of the Future 2020 and beyond.

"The common thread among all these jobs is making good – at long last – on HR's promise to connect people and business strategy to the new, exciting and lasting frontiers of the future of work," say Cognizant researchers, "all while amplifying what the greatest asset of any business (people) does best: be human." As Cognizant researchers highlight, "this is HR's moment of truth to lead the organization in navigating the future of work and prepare workers for the next decade."

What I feel that 5 HR Business Roles, which is expected out of CHRO's/Leaders in 2020 and beyond are.

1. Custodian of Healthy Organization

As HR leaders it is our utter more responsibility is to As HR professionals, it's our job to make peoples' working lives better. Going forward, this motivation will crop up in a number of specific roles, such as the **Chief Purpose Planner** or the **Workplace Environmental Architect**, who will "use his or her expertise in architecture, human-centered design, wellness, and public health to carry out the company's mandate to create a healthy and nurturing workplace environment."

"With the growth of the digital economy, our "always-on" way of working, the stresses in managing work-life integration, and now dealing with the coronavirus," well-being is evermore important,

2. Belive Officer

As more and more work is conducted virtually, HR will need to step in at every level to ensure trust and security remains intact between colleagues who are working remotely. "The proliferation of a "culture of data" increases that requirement, amplifying the need to create "human-in-the-loop" systems to ensure there is fairness, explainability and accountability within the senior leadership of HR," they say. Elsewhere, roles like the Human Bias Officer will work to foster a sense of inclusivity and belonging in the workplace, ensuing all employees are treated fairly.

3. Chief Innovator

Already, we're living in a profoundly altered world, one that requires entirely new modes of thinking about operations. This out-with-the-old mentality will lead to a number of Future HR roles. Professionals who can think on their feet, come up with creative solutions and innovate around the usual work arrangements and keep employees engaged, performing and motivated, will be in high-demand. "In a post-coronavirus world," Cognizant points out, "everything that can go virtual, will go virtual, from meetings to training workers," and roles such as the WFH Coordinator and the VR immersion counselors will address this transition.

4. Data base to Data Driven

Organization has to move from just Data base organization to Data driven organization. Data is the driving force behind many of the jobs on this list. Human Network Analysts "are expected to emerge" along with the HR Data Detective, channeling "their inner Sherlock" to "focus especially on trends with the greatest impact on business or HR goals." Furthermore, the Uni4Life Coordinator will use software that tracks data on how employees learn best then utilize algorithms to match them to courses. Gathering and using data ethically, securely and efficiently is going to form the bedrock of the vast majority of these Future HR roles. With large amounts of the working day conducted online, it will be easier than ever to gather this data. The "highest attention to ethical best practices is essential" in order to avoid "suffering from a "Big Brother" burden" i.e. too much intervention and employee surveillance.

5. Machine cannot supersede Human, but partner

Human and Machine partnership is very important As Cognizant says, "more and more technology pervades the work we do inside and especially outside of the HR function. And yet humans – and the notion of "essential workers" – have never been more integral to business than today." In other words, the future of work depends on humans and machines working in lockstep. Job number 12, the **Human-Machine Teaming Manager**, will be central to this movement, devising "an interaction system through which humans and machines mutually communicate their capabilities, goals and intentions."

6. Change Facilitator

As mentioned earlier in my book. The CHRO's role/Leaders role is to facilitate the changes Industry, environment and organization is going through. With the Covid19 Disrupting the whole world and business. The leaders should look at re-defining leadership, Facilitate Critical thinking rather than only sale growth. Coach and guide employees on how to deal or come out of an uncertain and disruptive crisis. Look at Technology Transformation @WFH norms/upskilling and influence employees with the mindset change from Survivor Guilt.

There are many new innovative roles which HR leaders should perform to make Organization a great place to work.

I will get there!...... What it take to reach my goal...

We all have motivations for achieving our goals whether it is personal goals or professional goals. We try doing whatever possible to reach our goals in life.

Whenever I and my family go for a long drive, I'm the one who used to drive car often. Always the Kids in the car used to ask after 2 to 3 hours of drive how long and I used to say few more kilometers to go. Of course, we always got there eventually, and we survived each trip. Guess kids were bit impatient.

I had a few personal and professional goals. Personal goals were to shape me well and burn a few calories. Started doing good exercise with some diet and for the first few months didn't see much results as many of them who are on way to lose weight would have felt so. After a few months I so my weight was reducing and I could feel my body was coming to some shape which I probably was expecting, then now what is next?. Similarly, I had a few professional goals to achieve and I heard myself asking "When am I going to get there?. I'm sure many of you ask yourself the same question when it comes to their goals to be achieved. Maybe you've been working so hard to get a particular result...and it just hasn't happened yet. If you ever find yourself in that position, here's a little encouragement and some points to reflect upon. Please understand, however, that nobody else has the answers to your challenges. These are some issues to consider, but it is you who ultimately must make your own decisions.

Passion for your Goals:- It is very important to re-assess your passion quotient. Are you still excited about attaining this goal? If so, keep forging ahead. However, if you have lost your enthusiasm for the goal, maybe it's time to re-evaluate the road you're on. You can fool yourself with rational arguments about why you're doing what you're doing. But I've learned that *gut feelings* don't lie. If every day is a struggle and brings little satisfaction, you're going to drain yourself physically, emotionally and spiritually. Careful here I'm not saying that every task along the way will be fun. That's rarely the case, But, if at the end of each day, you find yourself saying, " I hate doing this" you should think long and hard about making some changes.

Enjoy the Journey:- Some of us while traveling long distance is keen to see the milestone to find out how far we have reached but tends to miss the nice scenery along the way. And so it is with our lives. If we become too preoccupied with the results, we miss many of the precious moments that make up our days months and years. We don't appreciate our family and we don't see all of the beauty and miracles that surround us. So. Don't let the pursuit of your goal cause you to lose your balance and to shut out everything else in your world. Also, give yourself credit for the distance you've already traveled. We always focus on the things which we have missed, and we forget to appreciate the goals which we have accomplished. Think of where you were five to ten years ago... or even two years ago. Give yourself a pat on the back for the skills you developed, the commitment you've demonstrated, the lives you've affected, and the results you've achieved.

Patience is the essence of life:- Normally in our life one of the really important factors to make everything easy, and also to help us to have some kind of inner strength. Although our lives are like the waves of the ocean, they go up and down. Patience helps to work through all these ups and downs in our lives and even though life goes up and down, you can learn from them. These ups and downs of life may not become an obstacle for you if you practice patience. Sometimes for patience, we give example like water, water is flexible and soft but also very strong, Even rocks can be cut by water. But its nature is soft, calm, and very flexible, so Patience is like that. Years ago, Wayne Dyer said "Great things have no fear of time" what a marvelous approach! If you believe in yourself at the deepest level, you're going to continue until you accomplish what you set out to do. Sometimes, it will take much longer than you thought. As David Geffen once said, "There's God's plan and your plan. And your plan doesn't matter." Take the example of actor William H Marcy, who earned an Oscar nomination in 1997 for his performance in the movie Fargo. Macy's breakthrough came at the age of 47 after he had been acting for more than 25 years, mostly in plays. There were times he thought about giving up on his acting career. Now, he's in demand as one of the top actors in the business. So, hang in there and be patient.

Progress Gradually... It is so easy to get down and discourage when things aren't going as we had planned. And it's okay to get down...for a few minutes. Then, pick yourself up and make sure each day, to do a few things that will move you toward your objective. They don't have to be monumental tasks – even a phone call or a letter counts. This will keep your momentum rolling, and you will discover the rewards that come from being disciplined and taking constructive actions day in and day out. The worst thing you can do is sit back, do nothing, and feel sorry for yourself.

Be flexible and ready to take a detour... The best example would be during this period where the entire world is fighting Covid19, it becomes difficult for organizations and people to have long term goals. The markets, Businesses are very unpredictable the economy is unpredictable, so setting long term goals may not be a wiser thing to do. With this rapid change, however, comes incredible new opportunities, and we must be prepared to size them. That's why it is so important to be flexible about how you want to achieve your goals.. and perhaps even about your goals themselves. You must have the courage to change highways when the timings seem right. Often the path you planned to take is not the same one you'll wind upon. Be open to new possibilities!

Look for positive signs, however small:- There are days where you feel nothing seems to be going right. If things are happening to you for weeks and months, it's probably time to re-assess your strategy. But if you're making progress, even slowly, life will give you some signs, usually in the form of "minor" victories. You may close a significant sale...meet an important contact...or receive some gratifying feedback. Use these positive signs to inspire you to go even further!

Realize that getting "there" won't make you happy:- When u desperately wait for your new mobile set launch in the market for months and then the day it is in the market and you buy, after few days the excitement is gone. You were so excited before after you have got it excitement is gone after some time. It's easy to fall into this trap. You get so obsessed with achieving something in your business that you begin to get the crazy idea that reaching the goal will bring you instant happiness. Yet, the very moment of reaching your goal is seldom the euphoria you think it will be. Tennis star Martina Navratilova offered this insight: " The moment of victory is much too short to live for that and nothing else." You experience real joy and build a character from the entire journey toward and your goal. Besides, let's not forget that when you do get "there "you still must choose another "there "to pursue.

Few Guidelines to consider for you to arrive at and implement successful solutions to the critical issues in your life.

Believe in your abilities, and when you believe you can achieve it

Be-decisive –It is far better to choose one course and move forward. If your decisions don't work out, you can make adjustments or select a different option in the future.

Choose what is best for you - Make sure you're considering what is best for you.

Recognize the answers are often revealed step-by-step:- When you connect pieces of a puzzle you can see the big picture. So recognize each step and then you will see the next appropriate action to take.

Call from Inner self:- You should never ignore your intuition. Many times you would have felt something is going wrong, but you still went ahead. Chances are, you later regretted your decision. Your intuition tried to warn you that something is wrong, and you ignored it. Trust your intuition.

Be willing to implement the answer:- Most of us know answers to our problems, but are simply not willing to do what it takes to go forward with the solution. Recognize that your best answers will often involve challenges, obstacles, and, possibly, some emotional distress. That is the price you will have to pay. But in the long run, you'll be glad you did.

Read to Risk:- Courage is the one trait that will almost guarantee that you access your most powerful answers and implement them successfully. Have the courage to explore the limits of your potential and to act on the answer that emerges.

Spiritual Mind works well:- Many people find that they can access the "right" answers from their connection to a higher power. This isn't about pleading for a specific result. Instead, maintain an open mind and ask your higher power to guide you in making key decisions.

HR leaders/Leaders use the above guidelines to keep you on track and help you to see things from the right perspective. Remember, the journey is what counts. Be sure to cherish every step along the way.

Way to growth…… Don't miss enjoying journey, destination is near by…

It is often said your upbringing decides what kind of personality you develop into. True if a child's upbringing is with good values, culture, and education then you are supposed to be a good human when you grow up. When we're growing physically, we can see the changes. But when it comes to personal and professional growth, it is not always as easy to gauge our progress. There's no simple test we can take to assess personal growth. There are few signposts that we can use to gain insight into where we stand.

So how many of the following items are true for you now. If they are, not, try implementing these concepts as you strive to reach the next level in your self-development.

Don't fix blame or make excuses… You realize more and more that pointing the finger at others is not the answer to your problems. Instead, you take personal responsibility for your results and your happiness. Your focus on your attitude, your skills, your actions, and your discipline.

Build Practice …Practice your change process. You will brainstorm small, actionable practices that you can begin to fold into your habits and begin to create your Practice Treasury, a stable of behaviors that will help you bring to life the leadership Plan you designed.

Don't look back... Dwelling on unpleasant events in the past won't change them – and it only makes you feel rotten in the present. So why do it? Part of accepting personal responsibility is the recognition that, at any point. You can change the path you're on. Learn from the past, but don't obsess on it. Instead. Take action today to create a positive future.

You guard the sanctity of thoughts ... You no longer doubt that your thoughts are creating your reality. And, if that's the case, why would you ever think negatively? You're disciplining yourself to focus on what you want –as opposed to what you don't want.

Dig Deep – Reflect:- Reflect on your experiences to uncover your leadership beliefs and dig deep to uncover what makes you, you. In this step, you will uncover the life lessons that anchor your leadership and develop a deeper understanding of your unique personality and skillset.

Your spiritual beliefs are growing by leaps and bounds... Once you've accepted the fact that a higher power created you and has a specific plan for your life, you begin to live life at a different level. You tune into your possibilities and have faith that you'll receive guidance during your journey. You take bold action. And, you're finding that you have the strength to handle the setbacks and disappointments that temporarily block your path.

You stop comparing yourself with others:- You no longer judge your success by how much money someone else is making or how fast you climbed the ladder in your organization. You complete only with yourself and aim to develop your talents every day.

You have a sense of gratitude every day:- When you're young, you tend to take everything for granted-your health, the roof over your head, and the food on your plate. As the years go by, you suddenly experience the "darker" side of life. Either you or your relatives or friends face serious illnesses. You personally know people in their 30s, 40s, or 50s who die.

Instead of complaining about the things in your life that aren't perfect, you choose to be thankful for the many gifts you've been given. You identify with the sage advice of Eddie Rickenbacker, who once said, "If you have all the freshwater you want to drink and all the food you want to eat, you should never complain about anything."

You laugh a lot more – especially at yourself: - Several times each day, you find yourself letting out a hearty belly laugh. You take your work seriously but not yourself. Whether you're with clients, colleagues, friends, or family, make sure to laugh. You'll feel better and have a lot more fun.

You're excited about something. When you're living in the flow of life and up to your highest potential, you're enthused. You don't have to go around slapping people on the back, but you're upbeat and alive. You get up in the morning with a purpose and you look forward to the day's activities. People can just look at you or speak with you-and immediately pick up on your positive energy.

Taking Risk: - The path of growth demands that you venture into the unknown. That's where you discover yourself and find out what you're capable of achieving. You begin to get ideas and visions about great things you can accomplish, and you have the courage to go after them. Instead of just thinking about doing something, you take action and do it!

Should I bother about what others think?... Do you still need to get someone's approval before making a decision? On the path of growth, you're willing to do what you think is best for you- even if someone else won't like it. On fundamental issues such as your career, your relationships, and your goals, It's fine to get advice. But in the end, it's your view that counts. You'll never be happy following someone else's plan for your life.

Stop fixing others and take the opportunity to lift someone else...
Everyone has their own path to follow and that you don't decide the rate at which someone else progresses. So instead of "converting" others, you continue to work on yourself and find that your example is more powerful than any sermon you can preach. You know that you are where you now are, in large part, because some people believed in you... encouraged you...and helped you. You make a point to do the same for those who can benefit from your experience.

Logical perspective: - Your list of what's truly important in your life continues to shrink. You work hard and enjoy whatever material comforts you have, but things are not as essential to you as they once were. You recognize that the health and well-being of you and your loved ones is what really matters. You no longer let little day-to-day annoyances ruin your entire day.

How and Why?: - You've learned to tame your ego a bit and don't feel the need to always be the center of attention. You also realize that when you're talking, you're not learning anything. So, you balance your conversation and make sure to draw other people out by asking questions, How and why? You're more interested in learning about their backgrounds, their thoughts on various issues, their careers, and their families. Every person has a fascinating story to tell, and you want to hear it.

Mastering over a period:- To build physical fitness, you exercise several times each week. To develop a successful career, you pay attention to the basics day in day out. You're no longer looking for the " quick fix" Instead, you know full well that you must put in the effort before you can reap the reward. You find tremendous satisfaction in sticking with some-thing and mastering it over a period of time.

Rise your Bar:- You set high standards for yourself and others. Careful, this isn't about achieving "perfection" Rather on the path of growth, you simply have the desire to reach more and more of your potential. You no longer settle for less than your best effort. And, as you see more the potential in others, you encourage them to develop their talents as well.

To conclude the last chapter of **"Where should we go ahead"** we have to build trust and respect of employees in the Organization to make them future-ready and committed entrepreneurs. Leaders should analyze how they reach which they aspire to reach by defining the path of growth for themselves and the organization.

I would like to leave you with the thought that Organizations define Vision, Mission, and Values and expect employees to follow the same… But what can we Leaders do to make employees Vision/aspiration as Organization Vision/aspiration?... Think about it…

To conclude the last chapter of **"Where should we go ahead"** we have to build Trust and respect of employees in the Organization to make them future ready and committed entrepreneurs. I would like to leave you with the thought that Organizations define Vision, Mission and Values and expect employees to follow the same…But what can we Leaders do to make employees Vision/aspiration as Organization Vision/aspiration?...Think about it…

Industry Perspective

When asked with few leaders CEO'S/HR Heads this is what they had to say.

Is it true HR does what management wants them to do?

Respondent 1:-

I don't agree with this. Though there are organisations where HR is a dumped mouthpiece of the management and such Organization may gain some short term benefit but difficult to excel in long run.

I had a serious conflict with our HR Head on certain sanction while conducting monthly Town Hall. We had taken over a hotel, where most of the staff are working there since many years. Who never had high spent on employees' monthly Town Hall meet. While she proposed to convert that into more of a talent engagement programme of employees. I was little hesitant to sanction the budget as this was something not practiced for many years so why to increase the cost. But she managed to get that and today that turned out to be a major platform to create bond building among the team mates. It reduces individualism and increases good amount of coordination to improve our service efficiency and guest satisfaction.

Respondent 2:-

Yes and No. It varies from an HR leader to an HR leader. I have experienced three types of HR leaders:

1. Pleasing type: They believe that the only way to be on the good books of leaders/management is to say "yes," and as a result, they do what management asks them to.

2. Struggling type: They struggle to influence management for various reasons like -

    - Some have the brainpower, but they find it difficult to put across their point of views compellingly
    - Some lack business and financial acumen, and as a result, they can't offer a robust differing point
    - Some have not been able to build credibility as a business leader and remained only as HR leaders. Struggle to integrate solutions (keeping both people and business aspects in mind)

    In both these cases, the statement is true. However, the third type, which I call as

3. The HR—Business leader type, who is compelling, credible, and concise, along with strong knowledge of business and financials. They know the pulse of employees and hence can offer compelling solutions. Such leaders have their own personal, authentic leadership style. For such leaders, the statement doesn't hold good.

How can HR come out of the sandwich position (between employer and employee) and perform a clear mindset job role.

Respondent 1:-

I remember an incident where the management does not want to release a resource to another hotel of the same group because he was a productive sales guy for that hotel. He was offered more compensation in an unprecedented way to retain. HR manager tried to convince the GM to allow him to move, as his career progression will be better in terms of learning and he can be an asset to the group in coming days and also it exemplifies clear message to him of organization's selflessness, resulting a great sense of his loyalty to organization. His absence will create a short term crisis which can be managed in various ways. Unfortunately in spite of putting his best effort, HR manager could not convince the top management and the guy was not released. Although the guy was very keen to take the new opportunity for his learning purpose but under changed circumstances he took the salary hike and let go the opportunity. He has been poached by another competitor with similar salary but at a higher designation within 6 months which he was eyeing for in his Organization. It was an ultimate loss for the Organization and provide an additional edge to competitor. At times management must rely on long term benefit while ignoring short term agenda.

In this case HR would not have been sandwiched between management decision and his employees want/needs and if they would have listen to HR Manager. If organization can avoid such conflict and allow HR to function in an independent way for the resources assigned to him to the best interest of the organization, they can win the war at the cost of minor battle.

Respondent 2:-

Well, I don't think I will call it a sandwich position. Yes! HR has the responsibility to safeguard the organization and employee's interests. So, the role of HR is to strike the right balance between people and businesses. HR, like any other function, has to perform from a clear mindset job role. Why HR be different? If HR is playing the role of a strategic partner in a real sense, I firmly believe HR will not feel being in a sandwich solution.

You must have heard from many business leaders and functional leaders as HR doesn't understand business expectations and doesn't deliver as per management needs. So the third element what I'm going to speak in this book is about "Business leaders expectation from HR and What will make HR guys as good Business oriented leaders.

Respondent 1:-

To me the role of any business leader, is to organise and structure input in such a manner where expected output is profitable and sustainable. Me coming from Service industry, where biggest capital is Human Resource. Whether it is technology, automation or any other digital device for hospitality, it is an industry of guest servicing where human faces and gestures are irreplaceable. Hence HR manages the most critical capital of this business. Though the trend is changing with multinational players coming into the market, but Indian hotel business is still dominated by unorganised stand- alone hotels and resorts. Where most of the places HR Mgr. has been considered as mere transactional clerk to manage day to day attendance, leave and payroll. Very little or no emphasis being paid to involve them into business strategy building exercise, while officially they are custodian of their biggest capital. To me this is the largest Gap between a successful and failed Organization of hotel industry in our country. Human capital is different than any other capital in the business as it has got an individual thinking ability. Which made them more complex to manage. Behaviour of this capital is not uniform under similar circumstances. Therefore simple arithmetic of input output does not apply though all other variants remain constant. This is where the role of HR Mgr. comes. Who needs to be provided with holistic view of the business in terms of market, trend, product, competition, innovation and budget to map the best capital to suit the needs. They also need to think of future ahead of any other business leaders because it is the same capital who needs to be evolved, trained and innovate to combat the changes and stay in the business with support of all other capital.

Respondent 2:-

I have partly covered the response in my first question. HR has to become an HR-Business leader. They have a special responsibility to balance and integrate people and business aspects. To do so, HR leaders need to have their gravitas in place. They need to be compelling, credible, and concise, along with a solid understanding of the business model, knowledge of finance, and need to know the employee pulse at ground level.

HR needs to adopt a model whose outcome can be measured. For example, derive HR strategies to help achieve business objectives. HR should have a complete hold of workforce cost. HR should know the mechanism to enhance workforce productivity, ensure the right management in place, build leadership scorecards to measure performance and contribution, among others.

Conclusion

This book is about my experience and thoughts, yes of course I have spoken to few Industry leaders and HR leaders and have taken advice from many references mentioned below. This book will surely helps Leaders to understand and develop Human relations skills better, clear Myth and assumptions people have about Human resources function.

My idea is to bring the particle issues what a CHRO's/Human capital Head/Managers goes through in dealing with human capital and its challenges in the organization and what may be the possible solutions. There may be many more ideas which people may think is not covered in this book. Few may or may not agree with solutions or tips mentioned in the book, as everyone has their own perceptions. But the idea was never to describe solutions for all challenges in my first book.

Whatever may be the strategy of the organization, it is very important for the Organization to deal challenges and situation more humanly then tactically. Tactically may give you immediate results or may not, but dealing humanly with give organization a long mileage and make employees happy and trustworthy. Believe me that will serve your long term purpose. We all are hungry for three **"R" Respect, Recognition and Race** ... If the Organizations can give Respect and Recognition then third R i.e Response from employees for effective productivity will be assured. Another Mantra is as mentioned earlier treat people well they will treat the Organization always ...

I would like to Thank all my family members, who supported me to write this book during Covid19 lock-down, excusing me of doing all household stuff when we were off domestic help...:-) I would also like to Thank my friend and ex-colleagues for their thoughts and encouragements.

Thank you for your reading my Book. Please send your comments to my email ID on what did you like about the book and what you didn't like about the book. And of course your suggestions.

Email:- tuhinb1974@gmail.com

Name:- Tuhin Biswas

References

1. Harvard Business Review *"Are you a collaborative leader* "July-August 2011
2. Harvard Business Review *"How Management teams can have a Good Fight"* July-August 1997 by Kathleen M.Eisenhardt, Jean L. Kahwajy, and L.J.Bourgeois III
3. Swami Vivekananda's *Winning Formulas by* A.R.K Sarma
4. *The 7 Mantras for Peak Performance* by Major Gen Virinder Uberoy, page 226-231
5. Harvard Business Review May-June 1998 *The Necessary Art of Persuasion*
6. SwaPeter M. Senge, *The Fifth Discipline* (New York: Doubleday, 1990), p. 1.
7. Ikujiro Nonaka, "The Knowledge-Creating Company," *Harvard Business Review,* November–December 1991, p. 97.
8. *Transforming-the-Future*-The-CHRO-as-Chief-Change-Officer. pdf Heidrick & Struggles International, Inc.
9. *Building a Learning Organization* Harvard Business Review Jul-August 1993.
10. Better People Analytics, Paul Leonardi and Noshir Contractor Harvard Business Review
11. Book by Daniel Denson, Robert Hooijberg, Nancy Lane and Colleen Lief on *Leading culture change in Global Organizations*, chapter 1 *Building A High-Performance Business cuture.*
12. Peak Performance with Jamey Mroz, Mentor Box Audio video books
13. Robertsoncooper's *i-resilience reports* of Tuhin Biswas done during IMD programme.

14. Robert Howard, "The CEO as Organizational Architect: An Interview with Xerox's Paul Allaire," *Harvard Business Review*, September–October 1992, p. 106.
15. Modesto A. Maidique and Billie Jo Zirger, "The New Product Learning Cycle," *Research Policy*, Vol. 14, No. 6 (1985), pp. 299, 309.
16. Frank R. Gulliver, "Post-Project Appraisals Pay," *Harvard Business Review*, March–April 1987, p. 128.
17. David Nadler, "Even Failures Can Be Productive," *New York Times*, April 23, 1989, Sec. 3, p. 3.
18. Robert C. Camp, *Benchmarking: The Search for Industry Best Practices that Lead to Superior Performance* (Milwaukee: ASQC Quality Press, 1989), p. 12.
19. Roger Schank, with Peter Childers, *The Creative Attitude* (New York: Macmillan, 1988), p. 9.
20. Ramchandran Jaikumar and Roger Bohn, "The Development of Intelligent Systems for Industrial Use: A Conceptual Framework," *Research on Technological Innovation, Management and Policy*, Vol. 3 (1986), pp. 182–188.
21. TEDxAix talk of Vineet Nayar on book *Employee first customer second*.
22. Harvard Business Review - *We all need friends at work* ...by Christine M Riordam, July, 03, 2013
23. All my friends words and their thoughts,.*Other books and periodicals which was referred.*
24. Winning Attitude by Jeff Keller... chapters of When are we going to get there? The path of growth...

Made in United States
Troutdale, OR
01/21/2025